TUNE IN 2

Learning English Through Listening

Student Book

Jack C. Richards
& Kerry O'Sullivan

OXFORD

UNIVERSITY PRESS

OXFORD
UNIVERSITY PRESS

198 Madison Avenue
New York, NY 10016 USA

Great Clarendon Street, Oxford OX2 6DP UK

Oxford University Press is a department of the University of Oxford.
It furthers the University's objective of excellence in research, scholarship,
and education by publishing worldwide in

Oxford   New York

Auckland   Cape Town   Dar es Salaam   Hong Kong   Karachi
Kuala Lumpur   Madrid   Melbourne   Mexico City   Nairobi
New Delhi   Shanghai   Taipei   Toronto

With offices in

Argentina   Austria   Brazil   Chile   Czech Republic   France   Greece
Guatemala   Hungary   Italy   Japan   Poland   Portugal   Singapore
South Korea   Switzerland   Thailand   Turkey   Ukraine   Vietnam

OXFORD and OXFORD ENGLISH are registered trademarks of
Oxford University Press

© Oxford University Press 2007

Database right Oxford University Press (maker)

Library of Congress Cataloging-in-Publication Data

Richards, Jack C.
   Tune In: Learning English Through Listening / Jack C. Richards.
& Kerry O'Sullivan
      p. cm.
   Includes indexes.
   ISBN: 978-0-19-447109-1 (student book 2)
   ISBN: 978-0-19-447108-4 (student book 2 with CD)
   1. English language—Textbooks for foreign speakers. 2. Listening—Problems,
exercises, etc. I. Title: Learning English through listening. II. O'Sullivan, Kerry,
1952–. III Title.
   PE1128.R469 2006
   448.3'421-dc22

                                                        2006040033

Marketing Development Director: Chris Balderston
Senior Editor: Emma Wyman
Associate Editor: Hannah Ryu
Art Director: Maj-Britt Hagsted
Senior Designer: Mia Gomez
Art Editor: Justine Eun
Production Manager: Shanta Persaud
Production Controller: Eve Wong

Freelance Development Editor: Marietta Urban

STUDENT BOOK ISBN: 978 0 19 447109 1
PACK ISBN: 978 0 19 447108 4

Printed in China

Printing (last digit) 10   9   8

This book is printed on paper from certified and well-managed sources.

Acknowledgments:

Illustrations by: Harry Briggs: 22, 61, 88; Adrian Barclay/Beehive Illustration: 32, 37;
Dominic Bugatto/Three-in-a-Box: 43, 85, 89; Cybele/Three-in-a-Box: 32; Tony Forbes/
Sylvie Poggio: 16, 34, 58, 90; Guy Holt: 14, 38, 56, 71; Kevin Hopgood: 7, 46, 56, 64,
82; Katie Mac/NB Illustration: 10, 39; Karen Minot: 18, 19, 25, 26, 33, 49, 55, 70, 79;
Geo Parkin/American Artists Rep: 31, 52, 73; Lisa Smith/Sylvie Poggio: 8, 62, 91;
Glenn Urieta: 13, 23, 28, 42, 54, 67, 87; Bill Waitzman: 6, 76.

*We would like to thank the following for their permission to reproduce the photographs on the
cover and in the introduction*: Getty: Daniel Allen, (listening to music); Punchstock:
(raising hand in class); Punchstock: (whispering); Punchstock: (group of friends
jumping);; Punchstock: (talking on a cell phone); Punchstock: (holding a CD);
Punchstock: (student smiling).

We would like to thank the following for their permission to reproduce photographs: Alamy: Aflo
Photo Agency, 75; Cut and Deal Ltd, 57 (playing cards); Digital Archive Japan, 5 (dog
walking); Lebrecht Music and Arts Photo Library, 60 (autographed photos); Photo
Resource Hawaii, 79 (rainy day); Pictorial Press, 60 (The Beatles); Sportsweb, 41 (Ian
Thorpe); Travis VanDenBerg, 41 (Maria Sharapova); VStock, 78 (Japanese female);
Ardea.com: John Daniels, 62 (puppy); Thomas Dressler, 77 (drought); Francois Gohier,
50 (cat); M. Watson, 53 (bat); Barrett & MacKay Photo: 74 (spring); Bruce Coleman,
Inc.: Jacquelyn Foryst, 77 (Indonesian house); Joe MacDonald, 55 (hippos); CORBIS:
Theo Allofs, 53 (komodo dragon); Leland Bobbe, 9 (Asian female); Cloud Hill Imaging
Ltd., 17 (cells); C.Devan/zefa, 11 (laughing); Laura Doss, 29 (subway rider); Najlah
Feanny, 77 (flood); Aaron Horowitz, 77 (tornado); D.Hurst, 72 (phone); Simon Marcus,
2; SETBOUN MICHEL/CORBIS SYGMA, 79 (Mongolian boy); Mike Powell, 83; Helene
Rogers, 72 (ice cream maker); Ted Spiegel, 15 (orchestra); Simon Talpin, 2; Star/zefa,
89; LWA-Dann Tardlf, 9 (Hispanic female); Virgo/zefa, 57 (reading comic book);
Courtesy of Drs. Foster & Smith, Inc.: 72 (dog collar); Gallery 19: Gregg R. Andersen,
80 (Palm Pilot); Getty Images: AFP, 31 (SUV), 41 (Lance Armstrong), 51 (seeing-eye
dog), 77 (typhoon); altrendo images, 65 (friends in mall); Richard Bradbury/Taxi, 35
(shoes); Jim Cummins/Photographer's Choice, 29 (cyclist); Dorling Kindersley, 68
(jeans); Chad Ehlers/Stone, 30 (New Zealand landscape); Getty Images News, 68 (Razor
scooter); Getty Images Sport, 41 (Ichiro Suzuki, Michelle Wie);
GK Hart/Vikki Hart/The Image Bank, 51 (performing dog); Elke Hesser/Photonica, 36;
Frans Lemmens/Iconica, 55 (bird); National Geographic, 55 (blue whale); NBAE, 41
(Yao Ming); Rodrigo Ribiero/SambaPhotos, 59 (writing); Tom Servais/Workbook Stock,
59 (surfng); John Warden/Stone. 53 (koala); Phillip Wegener/Beateworks, 44 (house);
Chev Wilkinson/Stone, 11 (generous); Elizabeth Young/Stone, 59 (mannequin); Mark
E. Gibson: 47 (adobe house); The Hemera Collection: 68 (CD), 69; Janet Horton: 45,
59 (soda cans, puzzle); Jupiterimages Unlimited: Comstock Images, 5 (watching TV);
IndexOpen: Ablestock, 41 (boxing gloves), 62 (skateboard); 68 (skateboard, scotch
tape); Imagestate: Michel DENIS-HUOT/HOA-QUI, 53 (ostrich); Giovanni Lunardi, 35
(eyes); F.NICHELE/HOA-QUI, 77 (fog); Premium Stock, 17 (weights); Patrick Ramsey,
39; Kennan Ward, 53 (penguins); Inmagine: Bananstock, 5 (cooking), 65 (arcade), 9
(Caucasian male); Blendimages, 5 (checking e-mail); Brand X Pictures, 47 (houseboat),
63, 65 (haircut, ATM), 80 (café worker); Creatas, 27, 65 (woman eating); Comstock,
62 (sweater); Designpics, 12; Digital Vision, 15 (hiking), 51 (airport security dog), 77
(thunderstorm); 86; Epic Images, 84; image 100. 21; Image Source, 9 (Asian male),
30 (Christmas on beach), 35 (hair); Imageshop, 11 (crying); MIXA, 80 (two people
chatting); PhotoAlto, 5 (reading); Photodisc, 68 (contact lenses); Stockbyte, 35
(smile); THE KOBAL COLLECTION: 20th CENTURY FOX, 20 ("Fantastic Four"); ADC/
GRUPPO BEMA, 24 (woman playing violin); COLUMBIA/NEW LINE/FARMER, JON,
24 (Mr. Deeds); MIRAMAX/CANAL+/SOGECINE, 20 ("The Others"); TOUCHSTONE,
24 (Hidalgo); TOUHOKU SHINSHA, 20 ("Spirited Away"); TURNER NETWORK
TELEVISION/STAEDLER, LANCE, 62 (James Franco); UNIVERSAL/DNA/WORKING
TITLE, 20 ("Love Actually"); Map Resource: 26 (map); Minden Pictures: CARR CLIFTON,
74 (autumn); TUI DE ROY, 30 (Kiwi bird); TIM FITZHARRIS, 74 (winter); PETE OXFORD,
79 (Antarctica); MARK RAYCROFT, 50 (German Shepherd), 51 (farm dog); NPHA.
com: John Shaw, 79 (cloud); Omniphoto Communications: Bill Bachmann, 30 (Maori
couple); Jim Conaty, 47 (mansion); Grace Davies, 44 (apartment); Jeff Greenberg, 80
(volunteer); David Grossman, 78 (Caucasian male); Tom Stillo, 44 (dorm); OUP: Justine
Eun, 17 (calculus book), 35 (hands), 59 (camera), 60 (phone cards); Mia Gomez, 20
(movie stubs); Photo Edit, Inc.: Dennis MacDonald, 47 (trailer); Punchstock: Brand X
Pictures, 17 (test tubes, computer); Corbis, 14 (students), 78 (African-American boy);
Digital Vision, 81 (ice-skating); Image Source, 80 (sleeping in); Medioimages, 74 (tropics);
PhotoAlto, 3; Stockbyte, 81 (sick man); Thinkstock, 15 (play rehearsal); Randall Hyman:
47 (earth sheltered home); Robertstock: M. Barrett, 31 (couple); Karlene V. Schwartz:
65 (mall sign); Tangram Architekten: John Lewis Marshall, 48; Stevebloom.com: Steve
Bloom, 50 (chimpanzee), 53 (cheetah); Pete Oxford, 17 (frog); Uppercut Images: 2004
Plush Studios, 5 (ironing); Chase Jarvis, 59 (runner); Bert Wiklund: 77 (hailstorm);
Wildimagesonline.com: Martin Harvey, 50 (Africa Gray Parrot).

*The publishers would like to thank the following people for their help in developing this
series*: Sookyung Chang, Korea; Tina Chen, Taiwan; June Chiang, Taiwan; Robert
Dilenschneider, Japan; Bill Hogue, Japan; Hirofumi Hosokawa, Japan; Nikko Ying-
ying Hsiang, Taiwan; Yu Young Kim, Korea; Ellen Scattergood, Japan; Katherine
Song, Korea; Damien Tresize, Taiwan; Nobuo Tsuda, Japan; I-chieh Yang, Taiwan.
With special thanks to: Mark Frank, Japan and Su-wei Wang, Taiwan.

The publishers would like to thank the following OUP staff for their support and assistance:
Brett Bowie, Kaoru Ito, Kerry Nockolds, and Ted Yoshioka.

Introduction

Welcome to *Tune In!* This is a three-level listening series that teaches you the two important aspects of listening: understanding *what* people say and *how* they say it. This will help you improve your English.

Student Book

There are two lessons in each of the 15 units in the Student Book. Each lesson focuses on a different aspect of the unit topic. The lessons are organized into five sections, each one with carefully graded activities. This step-by-step approach makes learning natural English much easier.

BEFORE YOU LISTEN

This section introduces the topic of the lesson and presents key vocabulary for the listening activities.

LISTEN AND UNDERSTAND

There are two **Listen and Understand** sections in each lesson that go with recordings of people talking. The activities in these sections help you understand *what* the people say. These sections help you improve your overall listening comprehension skills.

For extra practice, you can also listen to the final **Listen and Understand** of each lesson on the Student CD.

TUNE IN

This section focuses on one feature of spoken English. This helps you understand *how* people say what they want to say. This will then help you speak English in a more natural way.

AFTER YOU LISTEN

This section gives you the chance to talk to your classmates about the lesson topic. It also lets you practice the feature of spoken English from the **Tune In** section.

Audio Program

There are various types of spoken English on the CDs—from casual conversations, class conversations, and voice-mail messages to weather forecasts, TV interviews, and radio shows. The complete audio program for the Student Book is on the Class CDs. There is also a Student CD on the inside back cover of the Student Book for self study. The Student CD contains the final **Listen and Understand** of each lesson. The track list for the Student CD is on page 92.

Scope and Sequence

Unit	Lesson	Lesson Objectives		Listening Genres
		Listen and Understand	**Tune In**	
1 The Family *Page 2*	1 Tell me about your family	▶ Understanding descriptions of families ▶ Recognizing similarities and differences	Expressing uncertainty	▶ Casual conversations
	2 It really annoys me	▶ Understanding routines ▶ Describing annoyances	Keeping conversations going	▶ Casual conversations
2 People *Page 8*	1 Tell me about yourself	▶ Recognizing qualities of people ▶ Identifying hobbies and interests	Asking for more details	▶ Casual conversations ▶ Newspaper interviews
	2 Who's your best friend?	▶ Identifying speakers' attitudes ▶ Recognizing time references	Giving more information	▶ Casual conversations ▶ Newspaper interviews
3 School Life *Page 14*	1 Why did you join a club?	▶ Making inferences from key words ▶ Understanding club activities	Expressing empathy	▶ Casual conversations
	2 Tell me about your classes	▶ Making inferences from context ▶ Identifying schedules	Expressing necessity	▶ Class conversations ▶ Appointment inquiries
4 Movies *Page 20*	1 What kind of movies do you like?	▶ Understanding recorded theater information ▶ Identifying likes and dislikes	Expressing disagreement indirectly	▶ Recorded theater information ▶ Casual conversations
	2 Tell me about the movie	▶ Identifying features of movies ▶ Identifying movie themes	Using conversation fillers	▶ School club conversations ▶ Casual conversations
5 Countries & Places *Page 26*	1 How was your trip?	▶ Identifying features of cities ▶ Understanding descriptions of experiences	Expressing pleasure or disappointment	▶ Class conversations ▶ Office conversations
	2 What's life like there?	▶ Identifying topics about countries ▶ Understanding descriptions of places	Asking for more details	▶ Casual conversations ▶ Radio show
6 Appearances *Page 32*	1 How tall are you?	▶ Identifying people from descriptions ▶ Describing preferences	Expressing preferences	▶ Model competition ▶ Dating agency interview & video introductions
	2 How do I look?	▶ Identifying features of people ▶ Distinguishing positive and negative opinions	Expressing opinions directly or indirectly	▶ Casual conversations
7 Sports *Page 38*	1 Do you like sports?	▶ Distinguishing speakers ▶ Identifying speakers' attitudes	Using double questions	▶ Survey interviews ▶ Casual conversations
	2 What do you think of boxing on TV?	▶ Distinguishing facts and opinions ▶ Understanding advice	Expressing agreement and disagreement	▶ Radio show ▶ Conversation with a coach
8 The Home *Page 44*	1 Where do you live?	▶ Making inferences from key words ▶ Identifying housing preferences	Showing interest	▶ Casual conversations ▶ Conversations with a housing officer
	2 What a fantastic home!	▶ Identifying features of homes ▶ Identifying topics about homes	Expressing enthusiasm	▶ Magazine interviews ▶ Radio show

Unit 1 The Family

LESSON OBJECTIVES
▸ Understanding descriptions of families
▸ Recognizing similarities and differences
▸ Expressing uncertainty

Lesson 1 Tell me about your family

1 BEFORE YOU LISTEN

What are your parents like? What are your siblings like? Check (✓) words in the list that describe them. Then compare your answers with a partner.

	Mother	Father	Brother or sister
1. quiet	☐	☐	☐
2. talkative	☐	☐	☐
3. sociable	☐	☐	☐
4. bossy	☐	☐	☐
5. stay-at-home	☐	☐	☐
6. active	☐	☐	☐
7. outgoing	☐	☐	☐
8. has a sense of humor	☐	☐	☐

2 LISTEN AND UNDERSTAND 🎧 CD 1 Track 02

A. School friends are talking about their families. Does each person come from a small (1 child), medium-sized (2 children), or big (3 or more children) family? Listen and check (✓) the correct column. The first one is done for you.

	Small	Medium-sized	Big
1. Jae-min	☑	☐	☐
2. Tara	☐	☐	☐
3. Ayumi	☐	☐	☐
4. Adam	☐	☐	☐

B. Listen again. Are these statements true or false? Write *T* (true) or *F* (false). The first one is done for you.

1. There are two boys in Jae-min's family. __F__

2. Tara's brothers are bossy. ___

3. Ayumi is younger than her brother. ___

4. Adam looks like his brother. ___

3 LISTEN AND UNDERSTAND 🎧 CD 1 Track 03

A. A teacher is asking some students about their families. Which parent does each student feel they are similar to? Listen and check (✓) the correct column.

	Mother	Father	Neither
1. Yu-ting	☐	☐	☐
2. Katherine	☐	☐	☐
3. Sang-woo	☐	☐	☐
4. Patrick	☐	☐	☐

B. Listen again. What is each student like? Circle the correct answer. The first one is done for you.

1. Yu-ting	**a.** outgoing	**b.** active	**c.** shy
2. Katherine	**a.** shy	**b.** sociable	**c.** quiet
3. Sang-woo	**a.** active	**b.** stay-at-home	**c.** bossy
4. Patrick	**a.** stay-at-home	**b.** outgoing	**c.** quiet

4 TUNE IN 🎧 CD 1 Tracks 04 & 05

A. Listen and notice how people express uncertainty.

> **A:** *Do you know what I mean?*   **B:** *I think so.*
> **A:** *Is your brother also a good singer?*   **B:** *I suppose so.*
> **A:** *Do you miss not having brothers or sisters?*   **B:** *I guess so.*

B. Now listen to other conversations. Is the person certain or uncertain about their answer in each conversation? Check (✓) the correct column.

	Certain	Uncertain
1.	☐	☐
2.	☐	☐
3.	☐	☐
4.	☐	☐
5.	☐	☐
6.	☐	☐

5 AFTER YOU LISTEN

A. Use this family tree as an example to draw your own family tree on a separate piece of paper.

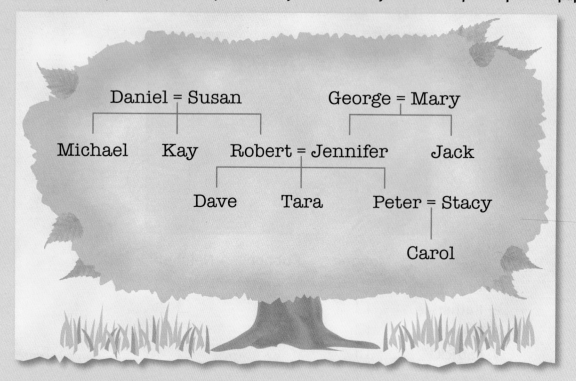

Daniel = Susan   George = Mary

Michael   Kay   Robert = Jennifer   Jack

Dave   Tara   Peter = Stacy

Carol

B. What is your family like? Complete this survey for yourself.

	Me	My partner
1. Is your family small, medium-sized, or big?		
2. Do you like the size of your family?		
3. How many brothers do you have?		
4. How many sisters do you have?		
5. Are they older or younger than you?		
6. What are their names?		
7. Do you have many aunts and uncles?		
8. Do you see them often?		
9. Do your grandparents live with you?		
10. What is your mother like?		
11. What is your father like?		
12. Are you more like your mother or father?		

C. Work with a partner. Take turns asking and answering the questions and complete the survey for your partner. Use this conversation to start but replace the highlighted parts with your own information.

A: *Is your family small, medium-sized, or big?*

B: *It's medium-sized.*

B: *Do you like the size of your family?*

A: *I guess so.*

Lesson 2 It really annoys me

1 BEFORE YOU LISTEN

A. How often do you do these activities when you come home? Check (✓) the correct column. Add two more activities of your own.

	Every day	Sometimes	Never
1. watch TV	☐	☐	☐
2. read	☐	☐	☐
3. check e-mail	☐	☐	☐
4. surf the Internet	☐	☐	☐
5. get dinner ready	☐	☐	☐
6. do household chores	☐	☐	☐
7. _____	☐	☐	☐
8. _____	☐	☐	☐

B. Choose an activity in part A that you like doing, don't mind doing, and dislike doing. Then compare your answers with a partner.

Like	Don't mind	Dislike
_____	_____	_____

2 LISTEN AND UNDERSTAND CD 1 Track 06

A. Friends are talking about what they do when they get home. Are these statements true or false? Write *T* (true) or *F* (false).

1. Marie uses her computer only to check her e-mail messages. ___
2. Shu-hua does not like talking to people when she is out with her dog. ___
3. Sumio's students are good at writing compositions. ___
4. Jennifer's favorite show is a cooking show. ___

B. Listen again. Do the friends like or dislike what they do at home? Check (✓) the correct column.

	Like	Dislike
1. Marie	☐	☐
2. Shu-hua	☐	☐
3. Sumio	☐	☐
4. Jennifer	☐	☐

③ LISTEN AND UNDERSTAND 🎧 CD 1 Track 07

A. People are talking about things that annoy them at home. Listen and check (✓) the thing that annoys them. The first one is done for you.

1. **a.** He has to go to bed by 9 P.M. ___
   b. He has to study until 9 P.M. ✓

2. **a.** His sister uses the phone a lot. ___
   b. His sister always borrows his cell phone. ___

3. **a.** She must be home before midnight on weekends. ___
   b. She is not allowed to meet friends. ___

4. **a.** Her parents come home late at night. ___
   b. She gets telephone calls late at night. ___

B. Listen again. What will each person say next? Circle the best answer.

1. **a.** What a pity. You missed a great game.
   b. Wow! You are really lucky.

2. **a.** So when is a good time to call?
   b. I didn't know you had a sister.

3. **a.** Oh, no! That means you'll miss my party tomorrow.
   b. So do you want to see a movie tomorrow night?

4. **a.** So when do you go to bed?
   b. Yeah, I guess that's all they can do.

④ TUNE IN 🎧 CD 1 Tracks 08 & 09

A. Listen and notice how people keep conversations going by asking follow-up questions.

> **A:** *What do you usually do when you get home?*
> **B:** *Well, I usually do my homework first.* **Don't you?**
>
> **A:** *What do you do when you get home?*
> **B:** *I always take my dog for a walk. I love dogs.* **Do you?**
>
> **A:** *Do you watch a lot of TV?*
> **B:** *Yeah, I do.* **And you?**

B. Now listen to other conversations and circle the follow-up question you hear.

1. **a.** Do you?   **b.** And you?
2. **a.** And you?   **b.** Don't you?
3. **a.** Do you?   **b.** Don't you?
4. **a.** Do you?   **b.** And you?
5. **a.** Don't you?   **b.** And you?
6. **a.** And you?   **b.** Do you?

5 AFTER YOU LISTEN

A. Match each picture with its correct label. The first one is done for you.

a.

b.

c.

d.

e.

1. Hey, turn that down! I'm trying to study. __b__
2. Hurry up! The show starts at 7:30. ___
3. Please pick up your things. Your room is a mess! ___
4. Who is calling so late at night? ___
5. Don't touch that! I'm watching this program. ___

B. How does your family annoy you? Complete this survey for yourself.

Does anyone in your family. . .	Me	My partner
1. spend too long in the bathroom?	_____	_____
2. play loud music when you are trying to study?	_____	_____
3. leave things lying around?	_____	_____
4. get phone calls late at night?	_____	_____
5. borrow your things?	_____	_____
6. not let you watch your favorite programs?	_____	_____

C. Work with a partner. Take turns asking and answering the questions and complete the survey for your partner. Ask follow-up questions to keep the conversation going. Use this conversation to start but replace the highlighted parts with your own information.

A: *Does anyone in your family spend too long in the bathroom?*

B: *Yes, my sister does. It really annoys me. And you?*

A: *No, not really. No one spends too long in the bathroom.*

LESSON OBJECTIVES
▸ Recognizing qualities of people
▸ Identifying hobbies and interests
▸ Asking for more details

Lesson 1 Tell me about yourself

① BEFORE YOU LISTEN

What are you like? Circle the words that describe you best. What other words would you use? Add two more words of your own. Then compare your answers with a partner.

1. I'm a pretty **easygoing** and **patient** person. I don't get angry very often.
2. I'm very **outgoing** and **sociable**. I love parties and meeting people.
3. I'm very **organized**. I don't miss appointments or forget things.
4. I'm **reliable**. I always keep my word. People can trust me.
5. I'm quite **serious**. I study hard and like to read many books.
6. I'm rather **shy**. I have trouble expressing myself and I'm quiet.
7. I'm very **creative**. I like to make new things.
8. I'm also _____ and _____.

② LISTEN AND UNDERSTAND 🎧 CD 1 Track 10

A. People are talking about themselves. Listen and circle the word that best describes them.

1. **Misaki**	**a.** organized	**b.** reliable
2. **Stacy**	**a.** sociable	**b.** shy
3. **Brendan**	**a.** reliable	**b.** easygoing
4. **Won-min**	**a.** sociable	**b.** serious
5. **Yusuke**	**a.** organized	**b.** easygoing

B. Listen again. Are these statements true or false? Write *T* (true) or *F* (false).

1. Misaki hates it when people miss appointments. ___
2. Stacy likes to talk to people she does not know. ___
3. Brendan cannot stand it when people change their minds. ___
4. Won-min does not like a lot of noise when she reads. ___
5. Yusuke often worries about things. ___

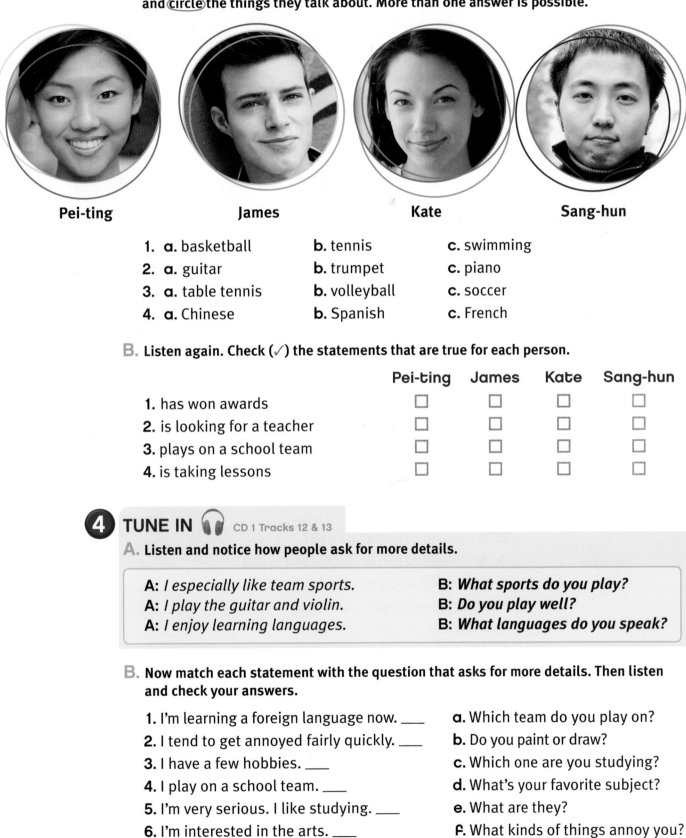

3 LISTEN AND UNDERSTAND 🎧 CD 1 Track 11

A. Students are talking about their hobbies and interests to a newspaper reporter. Listen and circle the things they talk about. More than one answer is possible.

Pei-ting   **James**   **Kate**   **Sang-hun**

1. **a.** basketball   **b.** tennis   **c.** swimming
2. **a.** guitar   **b.** trumpet   **c.** piano
3. **a.** table tennis   **b.** volleyball   **c.** soccer
4. **a.** Chinese   **b.** Spanish   **c.** French

B. Listen again. Check (✓) the statements that are true for each person.

	Pei-ting	James	Kate	Sang-hun
1. has won awards	☐	☐	☐	☐
2. is looking for a teacher	☐	☐	☐	☐
3. plays on a school team	☐	☐	☐	☐
4. is taking lessons	☐	☐	☐	☐

4 TUNE IN 🎧 CD 1 Tracks 12 & 13

A. Listen and notice how people ask for more details.

> A: *I especially like team sports.*   B: *What sports do you play?*
> A: *I play the guitar and violin.*   B: *Do you play well?*
> A: *I enjoy learning languages.*   B: *What languages do you speak?*

B. Now match each statement with the question that asks for more details. Then listen and check your answers.

1. I'm learning a foreign language now. ___
2. I tend to get annoyed fairly quickly. ___
3. I have a few hobbies. ___
4. I play on a school team. ___
5. I'm very serious. I like studying. ___
6. I'm interested in the arts. ___

a. Which team do you play on?
b. Do you paint or draw?
c. Which one are you studying?
d. What's your favorite subject?
e. What are they?
f. What kinds of things annoy you?

5 AFTER YOU LISTEN

A. What are you like? Complete this survey for yourself. Use the words in the box for questions 1 to 3.

shy	easygoing	patient	talkative	bossy	outgoing
active	creative	organized	reliable	serious	quiet

		Me	My partner
1.	What kind of student are you?	_____	_____
2.	What kind of friend are you?	_____	_____
3.	What kind of son or daughter are you?	_____	_____
4.	What sports do you play?	_____	_____
5.	What languages do you speak?	_____	_____
6.	What are you good at?	_____	_____
7.	What are you not so good at?	_____	_____
8.	What musical instruments do you play?	_____	_____

B. Work with a partner. Take turns asking and answering the questions and complete the survey for your partner. Ask questions for more details. Use this conversation to start but replace the highlighted parts with your own information.

A: *What kind of student are you?*

B: *I'm a serious student.*

A: *Do you study a lot at home?*

B: *No, not so much. I usually study at the library.*

LESSON OBJECTIVES
▸ Identifying speakers' attitudes
▸ Recognizing time references
▸ Giving more information

Lesson 2 Who's your best friend?

1 BEFORE YOU LISTEN

A. Match each quality with its correct meaning.

1. has a sense of humor ___
2. generous ___
3. direct ___
4. smart ___
5. punctual ___
6. emotional ___
7. optimistic ___
8. critical ___

a. can learn and think easily
b. shows feelings easily
c. thinks positively
d. says what they really think
e. enjoys jokes
f. ready to give things like time or money
g. arrives at the correct time
h. often says bad things about people

B. What qualities do you look for in a friend? Circle three in the list in part A and think of one more of your own. Then compare your answers with a partner.

2 LISTEN AND UNDERSTAND CD 1 Track 14

A. Friends are talking about people they know. Are they saying something positive or negative about the person? Listen and check (✓) the correct column.

	Positive	Negative
1.	☐	☐
2.	☐	☐
3.	☐	☐
4.	☐	☐
5.	☐	☐

B. Listen again. What will each person say next? Circle the best answer.

1. **a.** So that's why she's so popular.　**b.** I guess she's pretty boring.
2. **a.** He's not very generous.　**b.** What a nice friend!
3. **a.** Oh, that would annoy me too.　**b.** Well, she seems quite punctual.
4. **a.** I'm surprised he has any friends.　**b.** How nice!
5. **a.** She must be a lot of fun.　**b.** She needs to take things easy.

③ LISTEN AND UNDERSTAND 🎧 CD 1 Track 15

A. People are talking about their friends to a newspaper reporter. Are they talking about things they do now or things they used to do with their friends? Listen and check (✓) the correct column.

	Do now	Used to do
1.	☐	☐
2.	☐	☐
3.	☐	☐
4.	☐	☐
5.	☐	☐

B. Listen again. Are these statements true or false? Write *T* (true) or *F* (false).

1. The friends were both good horseback riders. ___
2. The friends do not always buy things. ___
3. The friends do not have anything in common. ___
4. The friends do not see each other very often these days. ___
5. The friends like similar kinds of movies. ___

④ TUNE IN 🎧 CD 1 Tracks 16 & 17

A. Listen and notice how people give more information when answering questions.

> **A:** *How well do you know Aoi?*
> **B:** *Pretty well, I guess.* **We've known each other for about a year.**
>
> **A:** *Do you have a lot in common?*
> **B:** *Yeah.* **We both like movies, especially action movies.**

B. Now match each question with its answer. Then listen and check your answers.

1. What do you think of Li-hong? ___
2. Does Chloe like going to parties? ___
3. Do you have any international friends? ___
4. Are your friends the same age as you? ___
5. Does your friend go to the same school as you? ___

a. Sure. My friend Tom is from Singapore.
b. Yes. We're in the same class.
c. Yeah. She often goes on weekends.
d. No, not all of them. Some are younger.
e. I like him. He's fun.

5 AFTER YOU LISTEN

A. Work with a partner. What things are important for people to become friends? Rank these statements from 1 (most important) to 7 (least important).

___ They are the same age.
___ They have similar personalities.
___ They like doing the same kinds of things.
___ They come from the same place.
___ They have the same sense of humor.
___ They like the same kinds of music.
___ They have similar opinions and beliefs.

B. What is your best friend like? Complete this survey for yourself. Add more information for each question.

	Answer	More information
1. Who is your best friend?	_____	_____
2. How long have you been friends?	_____	_____
3. Do you have similar personalities?	_____	_____
4. Do you both like the same kinds of music?	_____	_____
5. What things do you like to do together?	_____	_____
6. What things do you like to talk about?	_____	_____
7. What do you like the most about your best friend?	_____	_____

C. Work with a partner. Take turns asking and answering the questions. Use this conversation to start but replace the highlighted parts with your own information.

A: *Who is your best friend?*
B: *Kumiko, I guess. She lives in Tokyo.*
A: *How long have you been friends?*
B: *We've been friends for seven years. We were in the same class in junior high.*

LESSON OBJECTIVES
▸ Making inferences from key words
▸ Understanding club activities
▸ Expressing empathy

Lesson 1   Why did you join a club?

1 BEFORE YOU LISTEN

A. Which of these school clubs are you interested in? Circle the clubs. Then compare your answers with a partner.

1. drama club
2. English conversation club
3. painting club
4. photography club
5. international club

6. hiking club
7. dance club
8. orchestra club
9. hospital volunteer club
10. community volunteer club

B. Choose a club in part A for each statement.

a. It teaches me useful skills. ___

b. It develops my confidence. ___

c. It helps people. ___

d. It helps me keep fit. ___

2 LISTEN AND UNDERSTAND 🎧 CD 1 Track 18

A. Students are talking at school. Where are the conversations taking place? Listen and check (✓) the correct answer.

1. **a.** in the cafeteria ___
   b. in the auditorium ___
2. **a.** in the library ___
   b. in the gym ___
3. **a.** in the hallway ___
   b. in the teacher's office ___
4. **a.** in the classroom ___
   b. in the auditorium ___

B. Listen again. Circle the correct answer.

1. Su-jeong is interested in _____.
   a. lunch
   b. her parents
   c. plays

2. The student wants to _____.
   a. return something only
   b. return and borrow something
   c. borrow something only

3. Tae-min missed class because _____.
   a. he was ill
   b. he had club activities
   c. he had an appointment

4. The students _____.
   a. are at home
   b. attend a painting club
   c. are not in the same class

3 LISTEN AND UNDERSTAND 🎧 CD 1 Track 19

A. People are talking about school clubs. Which clubs are they talking about? Listen and circle the correct club.

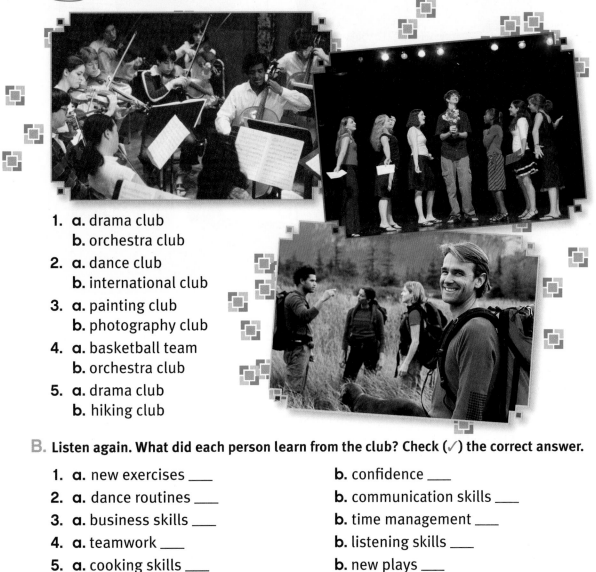

1. **a.** drama club
   b. orchestra club
2. **a.** dance club
   b. international club
3. **a.** painting club
   b. photography club
4. **a.** basketball team
   b. orchestra club
5. **a.** drama club
   b. hiking club

B. Listen again. What did each person learn from the club? Check (✓) the correct answer.

1. **a.** new exercises ___ **b.** confidence ___
2. **a.** dance routines ___ **b.** communication skills ___
3. **a.** business skills ___ **b.** time management ___
4. **a.** teamwork ___ **b.** listening skills ___
5. **a.** cooking skills ___ **b.** new plays ___

4 TUNE IN 🎧 CD 1 Tracks 20 & 21

A. Listen and notice how people express empathy.

A: *It was a lot of fun.* B: *Yes, it must have been.*
A: *It was hard work.* B: *Yeah, I bet.*
A: *It was a good experience.* B: *Yes, I'm sure it was.*

B. Now listen to other conversations. Check (✓) these expressions each time you hear them.

1. Yes, it must have been.   ___ ___ ___ ___
2. Yeah, I bet.   ___ ___ ___ ___
3. Yes, I'm sure it was.   ___ ___ ___ ___

⑤ AFTER YOU LISTEN

A. Match each statement with its response. Then practice the conversations with a partner.

1. My favorite is the dance club. It's a lot of fun. ____
2. When the dance club first started, it was very small. ____
3. The students in the club are really talented. ____
4. Dancing gives me energy for the rest of the day. ____
5. I was so out of shape when I first started dancing. ____
6. I hope I'll be dancing even when I'm old. ____

a. Yes, it must have been.
b. Yes, I'm sure they are.
c. Yeah, I'm sure it does.
d. Yes, I'm sure you will be.
e. Yes, I bet you were.
f. Yeah, I bet it is.

B. What is your favorite club at school? What is it like? Complete this survey for yourself. Add two more statements of your own about your club.

1. My favorite club is very _____.
2. When the club first started, _____.
3. The students in the club _____.
4. The club activities _____.
5. When I first started, I _____.
6. I hope I'll _____.
7. _____.
8. _____.

C. Work with a partner. Take turns making statements and agreeing with your partner. Use the conversations in part A as a model.

Lesson 2 Tell me about your classes

① BEFORE YOU LISTEN

Which subjects did you like at school? Which ones were you good at? Check (✓) the correct columns. Then compare your answers with a partner.

	Like	Good at
1. calculus	☐	☐
2. English	☐	☐
3. physical education	☐	☐
4. biology	☐	☐
5. history	☐	☐
6. physics	☐	☐
7. nutrition	☐	☐
8. literature	☐	☐
9. chemistry	☐	☐
10. drama	☐	☐
11. art	☐	☐
12. computer science	☐	☐

② LISTEN AND UNDERSTAND 🎧  CD 1 Track 22

A. Teachers are giving lessons. Which subject is each teacher teaching? Listen and number the subjects from 1 to 4. The first one is done for you.

a. nutrition ___   **b.** biology ___   **c.** English _1_   **d.** history ___

B. Listen again. Check (✓) the correct statement.

1. **a.** The teacher wants the students to write an essay. ___
   b. The essay should have five points. ___

2. **a.** Some foods can change the way we feel. ___
   b. Foods that are high in carbohydrates can make you feel tense. ___

3. **a.** The Great Wall of China was built about 1,000 years ago. ___
   b. The wall is over 6,000 kilometers long. ___

4. **a.** Frogs chew their food before they swallow it. ___
   b. Some frogs catch insects with their sticky tongues. ___

3 LISTEN AND UNDERSTAND 🎧 CD 1 Track 23

A. Students are making appointments. What are their class schedules like? Listen and number the schedules from 1 to 5.

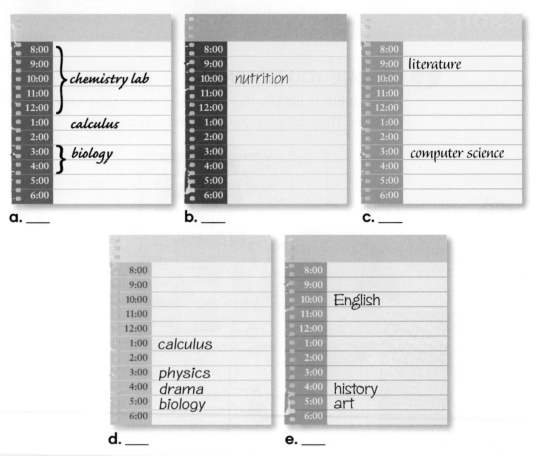

a. ___

b. ___

c. ___

d. ___

e. ___

B. Listen again. What time will the appointment be? Circle the correct time on the schedules.

4 TUNE IN 🎧 CD 1 Tracks 24 & 25

A. Listen and notice how people express necessity.

> *I **need to** check your assignment.*
> *I **have to** be in class all afternoon.*
> *We **should** play at five.*

B. Now listen to other conversations. Does the student think the activity is necessary or unnecessary in each conversation? Check (✓) the correct column.

	Necessary	Unnecessary
1.	☐	☐
2.	☐	☐
3.	☐	☐
4.	☐	☐
5.	☐	☐
6.	☐	☐

5 AFTER YOU LISTEN

A. **Role-play. You are planning your week at school. Choose five classes and two clubs in the boxes and write when you will go to them in your planner.**

physics	history	literature	biology
English	art	computer science	calculus

English conversation	dance	hiking
community volunteering	photography	drama

	Monday	Tuesday	Wednesday	Thursday	Friday
8:00					
10:00					
12:00					
2:00					
4:00					
6:00					
8:00					

B. **Work with a partner. You and your partner need to discuss a class project and also want to have a meal. Take turns arranging times to meet. If your partner is busy, ask about another time. Use this conversation to start but replace the highlighted parts with information from your planner.**

A: *Are you busy this week? We should discuss our class project sometime.*

B: *Yeah, I think we need to.*

A: *When would you like to meet?*

B: *Let's see . . . Are you busy Wednesday?*

A: *I have to go to my physics class from eleven to one. But my afternoon is free.*

B: *Why don't we meet around two o'clock?*

A: *Sure. That sounds good.*

B: *We should meet for lunch as well.*

A: *Yeah, I'd like that. Let's see . . .*

LESSON OBJECTIVES
▸ Understanding recorded theater information
▸ Identifying likes and dislikes
▸ Expressing disagreement indirectly

Lesson 1   What kind of movies do you like?

1 BEFORE YOU LISTEN

What do you think of these kinds of movies? Check (✓) the correct column. Then compare your answers with a partner.

	Like	Don't mind	Dislike
1. comedy	☐	☐	☐
2. action	☐	☐	☐
3. horror	☐	☐	☐
4. western	☐	☐	☐
5. science fiction	☐	☐	☐
6. animation	☐	☐	☐
7. musical	☐	☐	☐
8. romance	☐	☐	☐
9. drama	☐	☐	☐

2 LISTEN AND UNDERSTAND 🎧 CD 1 Track 26

A. Customers are listening to recorded information about movie theaters. Listen and check (✓) the correct statement.

1. **a.** The Korean movies are all comedies. ___
   b. The theater has a Website. ___

2. **a.** The *Star Wars* movies are showing on Sundays. ___
   b. The movies are for adults only. ___

3. **a.** The movies are American. ___
   b. Information about show times is only in the newspaper. ___

4. **a.** The movies are from the 1950s. ___
   b. The theater is showing five movies a day. ___

B. Listen again. Check (✓) the statements that are true for each theater.

	Star	Rex	Royal	Sun
1. has movies with subtitles	☐	☐	☐	☐
2. has action movies	☐	☐	☐	☐
3. has special prices	☐	☐	☐	☐
4. has science fiction movies	☐	☐	☐	☐
5. has new movies	☐	☐	☐	☐

③ LISTEN AND UNDERSTAND 🎧 CD 1 Track 27

A. Friends are talking about movies. How often does each person go to the movies? Listen and match each person with the correct statement.

1. Akira ___   **a.** She goes to the movies once in a while.
2. Sam ___   **b.** He does not go to the movies often.
3. Jane ___   **c.** She goes to the movies often.
4. Julia ___   **d.** He goes to the movies very often.

B. Listen again. Do the friends like the same or different kinds of movies? Circle the correct answer.

1. **a.** same   **b.** different
2. **a.** same   **b.** different
3. **a.** same   **b.** different
4. **a.** same   **b.** different

④ TUNE IN 🎧 CD 1 Tracks 28 & 29

A. Listen and notice how people express disagreement indirectly.

> A: *I think horror movies are great. Don't you?*
>
> A: *There are so many great movies out these days.*
>
> B: **Yeah,** *some are good,* **but** *most seem silly.*
> B: *I guess so, but I like comedies better.*
>
> B: **Really? Do you think so?**
> B: **Well, maybe, but** *I prefer older movies.*

B. Now listen to other conversations. Does the person express agreement or disagreement in each conversation? Check (✓) the correct column.

	Agreement	Disagreement
1.	☐	☐
2.	☐	☐
3.	☐	☐
4.	☐	☐
5.	☐	☐
6.	☐	☐

5 AFTER YOU LISTEN

A. **What do you think about movies? Complete this survey for yourself.**

	Me	Student 1	Student 2
1. the best action movie	_____	_____	_____
2. the scariest movie	_____	_____	_____
3. the best animated movie	_____	_____	_____
4. the best romantic movie	_____	_____	_____
5. the movie you cried in the most	_____	_____	_____
6. the movie you laughed in the most	_____	_____	_____
7. the best movie ever	_____	_____	_____
8. the worst movie ever	_____	_____	_____
9. the best actor from your country	_____	_____	_____
10. the best actress from your country	_____	_____	_____

B. **Work in groups of three. Take turns asking and answering the questions and complete the survey for your partners. Use these conversations but replace the highlighted parts with your own information. How many of your answers are the same?**

A: *What do you think is the best action movie?*
B: *I think it's Batman Begins.*
C: *Really? Do you think so? I think the first Batman is better.*

B: *What do you think is the best romantic movie?*
C: *I think it's Titanic.*
A: *Well, maybe, but I prefer Love Actually.*

C: *Who do you think is the best actress from your country?*
A: *I think it's Ziyi Zhang.*
B: *Yeah, I guess she's good, but I think Gong Li is better.*

LESSON OBJECTIVES
▸ Identifying features of movies
▸ Identifying movie themes
▸ Using conversation fillers

Lesson 2 Tell me about the movie

① BEFORE YOU LISTEN

Number the movie events in the correct order. The first one is done for you. Then compare your answers with a partner. What kind of movie is it?

____ Unfortunately, the boy is sent off to defend his country in a war.

____ They lose contact with each other after the war is over.

____ And then they decide to get married.

____ Then, a few years later, they meet by chance.

_1_ A boy and a girl become childhood sweethearts.

____ They renew their friendship.

____ After they get married, they move to Hawaii.

② LISTEN AND UNDERSTAND 🎧 CD 1 Track 30

A. Movie club members are talking about movies to include in a film festival. Which features of movies do they mention? Listen and check (✓) the features.

	Story	Actor(s)	Music	Special effects
1.	☐	☐	☐	☐
2.	☐	☐	☐	☐
3.	☐	☐	☐	☐
4.	☐	☐	☐	☐

B. Listen again. Is the movie included in the festival? Circle the correct answer.

1. **a.** Yes   **b.** No
2. **a.** Yes   **b.** No
3. **a.** Yes   **b.** No
4. **a.** Yes   **b.** No

3 LISTEN AND UNDERSTAND 🎧 CD 1 Track 31

A. Friends are talking about movies they saw on the weekend. Listen and check (✓) the correct statement.

1. **a.** A man inherits a lot of money but then loses it all. ___
   b. At the end of the movie, he gets all his money back. ___

2. **a.** A woman becomes a famous musician. ___
   b. She has a very long and successful career. ___

3. **a.** A man and a woman meet on a boat. ___
   b. The story involves a lot of exciting action. ___

4. **a.** The whale is sad and lonely at the theme park. ___
   b. The people buy the theme park. ___

5. **a.** A cowboy tries to help people in the city. ___
   b. A rich farmer wants to take the people's land. ___

B. Listen again. Did each movie have a happy or sad ending? Check (✓) the correct column.

	🙂	🙁
1.	☐	☐
2.	☐	☐
3.	☐	☐
4.	☐	☐
5.	☐	☐

4 TUNE IN 🎧 CD 1 Tracks 32 & 33

A. Listen and notice how people use conversation fillers.

A: What's that movie about?	B: **Um . . . I think** it's a true story.
	B: **Uh . . . well** it's about this guy.
	B: **Um . . . let me think** . . . It's a comedy.
	B: **Let's see** . . . It's actually about animals.

B. Now listen to other conversations and circle the conversation filler you hear.

1. **a.** Um . . . I think
   b. Let's see . . .

2. **a.** Let's see . . .
   b. Um . . . let me think . . .

3. **a.** Um . . . I think
   b. Uh . . . well

4. **a.** Um . . . let me think . . .
   b. Um . . . I think

5. **a.** Uh . . . well
   b. Let's see . . .

5 AFTER YOU LISTEN

A. How well do you know movies? Choose the correct answer in the boxes for each question.

King Kong	Jaws	The Academy Awards	Star Wars	Jackie Chan
Shrek	Tom Cruise	Beyoncé Knowles	Spider-Man	Titanic

1. What is the name of the movie about a famous ship that sank? _____

2. Which singer is also a movie star? _____

3. Which actor plays the main character in the *Mission: Impossible* movies? _____

4. What is the name of the movie about a huge gorilla? _____

5. What is the science fiction movie series about the Jedi? _____

6. What is the name of the animated movie about a large green monster? _____

7. What is the name of the movie about a hero who can swing from buildings? _____

8. What is the name of the most famous prize given for movies in Hollywood? _____

9. What is the name of the movie about a shark? _____

10. Which actor plays a main character in the *Rush Hour* movies? _____

B. Work with a partner. Take turns asking and answering the questions in part A. Use conversation fillers if you are not sure about an answer. Use this conversation as a model. Then check your answers below.

A: *What is the name of the movie about a famous ship that sank?*
B: *Um . . . let me think . . . Is it Jaws?*

C. Work with a partner. Write three movie questions of your own and take turns asking and answering the questions. Who had the most correct answers?

	Question	Answer
1.	_____	_____
2.	_____	_____
3.	_____	_____

Answers: 1. Titanic, 2. Beyoncé Knowles, 3. Tom Cruise, 4. King Kong, 5. Star Wars, 6. Shrek, 7. Spider-Man 8. The Academy Awards, 9. Jaws, 10. Jackie Chan

LESSON OBJECTIVES
▸ Identifying features of cities
▸ Understanding descriptions of experiences
▸ Expressing pleasure or disappointment

Lesson 1 · How was your trip?

1 BEFORE YOU LISTEN

A. Are these names of countries or continents? Check (✓) the correct column. Then compare your answers with a partner.

	Country	Continent
1. Africa	☐	☐
2. Asia	☐	☐
3. Brazil	☐	☐
4. China	☐	☐
5. Europe	☐	☐
6. Japan	☐	☐
7. North America	☐	☐
8. South Africa	☐	☐
9. South America	☐	☐
10. South Korea	☐	☐
11. Spain	☐	☐
12. Thailand	☐	☐

B. Think of a city in each country. Then compare your answers with a partner.

2 LISTEN AND UNDERSTAND 🎧 CD 1 Track 34

A. Students are giving a class presentation about where they come from. Listen and check (✓) the correct city on each map.

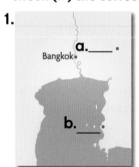

1. Bangkok• a.____ • b.____

2. a.____ • b.____ •Rio de Janeiro

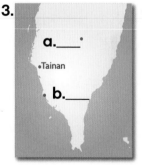

3. a.____ • •Tainan b.____

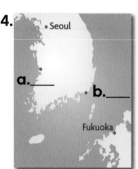

4. •Seoul a.____ b.____ Fukuoka

B. Listen again. Which topic does each student talk about? Circle the correct topic.

1. **Somchai**	a. cost of living	b. climate	c. food
2. **Luis**	a. climate	b. employment	c. language
3. **Ya-ping**	a. industry	b. size	c. cost of living
4. **Jae-won**	a. size	b. language	c. food

③ LISTEN AND UNDERSTAND 🎧 CD 1 Track 35

A. Office coworkers are talking about places they have visited. Did they like or dislike each place? Circle the correct word.

1. **a.** like   **b.** dislike
2. **a.** like   **b.** dislike
3. **a.** like   **b.** dislike
4. **a.** like   **b.** dislike
5. **a.** like   **b.** dislike

B. Listen again. Check (✓) the correct statement.

1. **a.** She visited Hong Kong in June. ___
   b. She found prices too high. ___
2. **a.** He went to New Zealand in the winter. ___
   b. He spent one week there. ___
3. **a.** She had been to Taiwan before. ___
   b. She bought things in Taipei. ___
4. **a.** The weather in London was hot. ___
   b. People told him to visit in the spring. ___
5. **a.** He found that Tokyo was easy to get around. ___
   b. He thought that Tokyo was not interesting. ___

④ TUNE IN 🎧 CD 1 Tracks 36 & 37

A. Listen and notice how people express pleasure or disappointment.

	Pleasure	Disappointment
I went to New Zealand last summer.	***That's great!***	
Everyone I met was so nice.	***That's terrific!***	
I really had a great time.	***That's nice.***	
It was very hot and humid.		***What a pity.***
The prices were too high.		***That's too bad.***
I found London very expensive.		***What a shame.***

B. Now listen to other conversations. Does the person express pleasure or disappointment in each conversation? Check (✓) the correct column.

	Pleasure	Disappointment
1.	☐	☐
2.	☐	☐
3.	☐	☐
4.	☐	☐
5.	☐	☐
6.	☐	☐

⑤ AFTER YOU LISTEN

A. Choose expressions in the box to complete the conversation. Then practice the conversation with a partner.

What a pity.	That's nice.	That's great.	That's too bad.
What a shame.	That's wonderful.	That's terrific.	That's terrible.

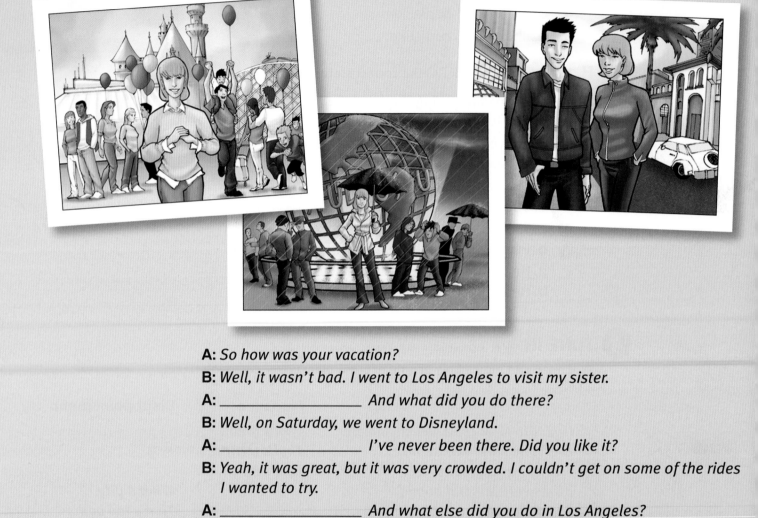

A: *So how was your vacation?*

B: *Well, it wasn't bad. I went to Los Angeles to visit my sister.*

A: _____ *And what did you do there?*

B: *Well, on Saturday, we went to Disneyland.*

A: _____ *I've never been there. Did you like it?*

B: *Yeah, it was great, but it was very crowded. I couldn't get on some of the rides I wanted to try.*

A: _____ *And what else did you do in Los Angeles?*

B: *We went to Universal Studios.*

A: _____ *Did you enjoy it? I hear it's amazing.*

B: *Yes, it is. But, unfortunately, the weather wasn't very nice on Sunday. It was cold and wet.*

A: _____ *It can get cold sometimes at this time of the year.*

B: *But anyway, I enjoyed it. And guess what? I ran into an old friend of mine that I hadn't seen in ten years.*

A: _____ *It sounds like you had a pretty good vacation then.*

B: *Yes, I did.*

B. Work with a partner. Talk about your last vacation. Take turns asking and answering questions about what you did. Use the conversation in part A as a model.

LESSON OBJECTIVES
▸ Identifying topics about countries
▸ Understanding descriptions of places
▸ Asking for more details

Lesson 2 What's life like there?

1 BEFORE YOU LISTEN

A. What is life in your country like? Circle the statements that are true. Then compare your answers with a partner.

Topic	Statement
1. family life	Most families have two children.
2. food	People eat rice every day.
3. free time	Hiking is a popular leisure activity.
4. transportation	People travel to work or school by bicycle.
5. housing	Most people live in apartments.
6. employment	Unemployment is quite low.
7. education	Public schools are very good.
8. health	Public hospitals are free.

B. Work with a partner. Change the statements that are not circled so they are true for your country.

2 LISTEN AND UNDERSTAND 🎧 CD 1 Track 38

A. Students at a language school are talking about life in their home countries. Which topics do they talk about? Listen and circle the correct topic.

1. **a.** housing   **b.** employment
2. **a.** education   **b.** food
3. **a.** health   **b.** family life
4. **a.** family life   **b.** transportation
5. **a.** free time   **b.** education

B. Listen again. Check (✓) the correct statement.

1. **a.** People do not usually buy a house. ____
   b. Apartments are not very popular. ____

2. **a.** Children learn English from the age of seven. ____
   b. Most people send their children to public schools. ____

3. **a.** Grandparents often live alone. ____
   b. Both parents usually work. ____

4. **a.** There is a good subway system. ____
   b. Most people drive cars. ____

5. **a.** Young people enjoy gardening. ____
   b. Children enjoy the same things as kids in other countries. ____

3 LISTEN AND UNDERSTAND 🎧 CD 1 Track 39

A. A guest on a radio show is talking about New Zealand. Does she give information about these questions? Check (✓) the correct column.

	Yes	No
1. How many people live there?	☐	☐
2. What kind of people live there?	☐	☐
3. Why are people called Kiwis?	☐	☐
4. What traditional dishes are there?	☐	☐
5. What dangerous animals live there?	☐	☐
6. What is the scenery like?	☐	☐
7. What is the climate like?	☐	☐
8. What is the education system like?	☐	☐

B. Listen again. Are these statements true or false? Write *T* (true) or *F* (false).

1. New Zealand is much bigger than Japan. ___

2. Most of the population are Maori. ___

3. Kiwi birds are not common. ___

4. Half of New Zealand is natural forest. ___

5. New Zealand is warm in August. ___

4 TUNE IN 🎧 CD 1 Tracks 40 & 41

A. Listen and notice how people ask for more details.

> **A:** *Well, gardening is popular with older people.*
> **B:** *Oh? And what about children?*
>
> **A:** *Only about four million people live in New Zealand.*
> **B:** *Really? And are most of the people originally from England?*
>
> **A:** *Well, it's the name of our most famous bird.*
> **B:** *Uh-huh. What kind of bird is it?*

B. Now listen to other conversations. Which topic does the person ask about when asking for more details in each conversation? Check (✓) the correct topic.

1. **a.** size ___   **b.** price ___

2. **a.** famous people ___   **b.** soccer ___

3. **a.** work ___   **b.** cars ___

4. **a.** public schools ___   **b.** private schools ___

5. **a.** work hours ___   **b.** vacations ___

5 AFTER YOU LISTEN

A. Put these sentences in order to make a conversation. Then practice the conversation with a partner.

___ *Wow, for every meal? Do you eat it for breakfast too?*

___ *My favorite is brown rice.*

___ *Sure, there's white rice, brown rice, and sticky rice, for example.*

___ *Tell me about the food in your country. What do you eat every day?*

___ *Sure, we eat it in the morning too. But we eat it with other dishes.*

___ *Oh? What kind of dishes do you eat it with?*

___ *We eat rice every day and, traditionally, for every meal.*

___ *Wow, that's a lot of dishes! And do you have different kinds of rice?*

___ *Really? I didn't know there were many different kinds. What's your favorite?*

___ *Let's see. We normally have it with vegetable dishes, soup, and meat dishes.*

B. Work with a partner. Decide who is student A and who is student B. Read the statements about life in the US in your box. Think about how your country is different.

Student A

Cars: Most families in the US have at least one car. Big cars, like sport utility vehicles and trucks, are popular.

Student B

Family life: Most families in the US do not live with grandparents. Children usually leave their home after high school and live alone.

C. Role-play. Work with a partner. Your partner is a visitor from the US and you are giving information about your country. Take turns asking and answering questions. Use the conversation in part A as a model.

Unit
6 Appearances

LESSON OBJECTIVES
▸ Identifying people from descriptions
▸ Describing preferences
▸ Expressing preferences

Lesson 1   How tall are you?

1 BEFORE YOU LISTEN

Match each person with the correct description. Then compare your answers with a partner.

1. He is quite short and is about 20 years old. ____

2. He is very tall and middle-aged. ____

3. She is fairly short and in her early teens. ____

4. He is of medium height and in his 30s. ____

5. She is pretty tall and in her mid-20s. ____

2 LISTEN AND UNDERSTAND 🎧 CD 2 Track 02

A. A host for a male model competition is introducing contestants. Listen and number the contestants from 1 to 5.

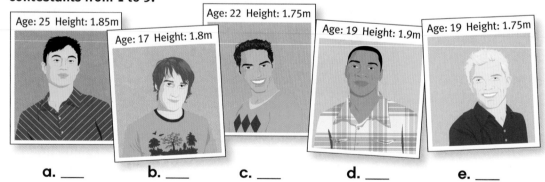

Age: 25 Height: 1.85m
Age: 17 Height: 1.8m
Age: 22 Height: 1.75m
Age: 19 Height: 1.9m
Age: 19 Height: 1.75m

a. ____   b. ____   c. ____   d. ____   e. ____

B. Listen again. Check (✓) the statements that are true for each contestant.

	David	Andrew	Justin	Steven	Ben
1. is a student	☐	☐	☐	☐	☐
2. has modeled before	☐	☐	☐	☐	☐
3. is from the US	☐	☐	☐	☐	☐

3 LISTEN AND UNDERSTAND 🎧 CD 2 Tracks 03 & 04

A. Dylan is at a dating agency. What kind of person does he prefer to date? Listen and check (✓) the correct answer.

Age		Height		Personality		Interests	
under 20	☐	under 1.7m	☐	serious	☐	sports	☐
mid-20s	☐	over 1.7m	☐	reliable	☐	movies	☐
over 20	☐	not important	☐	outgoing	☐	music	☐

B. Now listen to women introducing themselves by video. Which woman is the best date for Dylan? Circle the best woman.

1. Lucy   **2.** An-yi   **3.** Jessica   **4.** Atsuko

4 TUNE IN 🎧 CD 2 Tracks 05 & 06

A. Listen and notice how people express preferences.

> **A:** *What kind of woman would you like to date?* **B:** *I'd prefer someone younger.*
> **A:** *Do you prefer someone about your height?* **B:** *I prefer shorter girls, actually.*

B. Now listen to other conversations. Does the person say *I prefer* or *I'd prefer* in each conversation? Check (✓) the correct column.

	I prefer	*I'd prefer*
1.	☐	☐
2.	☐	☐
3.	☐	☐
4.	☐	☐
5.	☐	☐
6.	☐	☐

5 AFTER YOU LISTEN

A. What kind of person do you prefer to date? Complete this survey for yourself. Add two more qualities of your own and check (✓) your preferences.

	Me	My partner
1. older	☐	☐
2. younger	☐	☐
3. the same age	☐	☐
4. shorter	☐	☐
5. taller	☐	☐
6. the same height	☐	☐
7. very good looking	☐	☐
8. average looking	☐	☐
9. concerned about their appearance	☐	☐
10. unconcerned about their appearance	☐	☐
11. sociable	☐	☐
12. stay-at-home	☐	☐
13. quiet	☐	☐
14. talkative	☐	☐
15. active	☐	☐
16. serious	☐	☐
17. carefree	☐	☐
18. _____	☐	☐
19. _____	☐	☐

B. Work with a partner. Take turns asking and answering the questions and complete the survey for your partner. Use these conversations to start but replace the highlighted parts with your own information. How many of your preferences are the same?

A: *Would you prefer someone older than you?*

B: *Yes, I would. I'd prefer someone much older.*

A: *I would too.*

B: *Do you prefer someone taller than you?*

A: *No, I don't. I prefer someone shorter.*

B: *You do? I prefer someone the same height as me.*

LESSON OBJECTIVES
▸ Identifying features of people
▸ Distinguishing positive and negative opinions
▸ Expressing opinions directly or indirectly

Lesson 2 How do I look?

1 BEFORE YOU LISTEN

What do you notice when you meet someone for the first time? Rank this list from 1 (most noticed) to 8 (least noticed). Then compare your answers with a partner.

___ smile

___ teeth

___ clothes

___ eyes

___ shoes

___ hands

___ body

___ hairstyle

2 LISTEN AND UNDERSTAND 🎧 CD 2 Track 07

A. People are talking about their first impressions of others. What did they notice first? Listen and circle the correct feature.

1. **a.** eyes   **b.** lips   **c.** hands
2. **a.** teeth   **b.** hands   **c.** feet
3. **a.** body   **b.** eyes   **c.** clothes
4. **a.** shoes   **b.** hairstyle   **c.** legs
5. **a.** smile   **b.** body   **c.** hands

B. Listen again. Are these statements true or false? Write *T* (true) or *F* (false).

1. Stacy is wearing colored contacts. ___
2. Kenta plays the piano. ___
3. Elizabeth looks good today. ___
4. Gina has short hair. ___
5. Wen-ping's boyfriend exercises a lot. ___

3 LISTEN AND UNDERSTAND 🎧 CD 2 Track 08

A. People are asking friends about the way they look. Does each friend give a positive opinion or a negative opinion? Listen and check (✓) the correct column.

	Positive	Negative
1.	☐	☐
2.	☐	☐
3.	☐	☐
4.	☐	☐

B. Listen again. What advice will each friend give next? Check (✓) the best answer.

1. **a.** You should have short hair. ____
   b. You should have long hair. ____
2. **a.** You should wear a nice jacket too. ____
   b. You should wear sneakers. ____
3. **a.** You should wear this style more often. ____
   b. You should exchange them for a different style. ____
4. **a.** You should try jogging. ____
   b. You should try to eat a lot. ____

4 TUNE IN 🎧 CD 2 Tracks 09 & 10

A. Listen and notice how people express opinions directly or indirectly.

What do you think of my new hairstyle?

Directly	Indirectly
I don't think it looks good on you.	***If you ask me,*** *I don't think it looks good on you.*
It makes you look too old.	***I think that*** *it makes you look too old.*
It's too short for you.	***It seems like*** *it's too short for you.*
I don't really like it.	***To be honest,*** *I don't really like it.*

B. Now listen to other conversations. Does the person express their opinion directly or indirectly in each conversation? Circle the correct answer.

1. **a.** directly   **b.** indirectly
2. **a.** directly   **b.** indirectly
3. **a.** directly   **b.** indirectly
4. **a.** directly   **b.** indirectly
5. **a.** directly   **b.** indirectly
6. **a.** directly   **b.** indirectly

5 AFTER YOU LISTEN

A. Work with a partner. What should these people do to make themselves look better? Suggest two things each person can change and give one reason for each of the changes.

Mitsuki   Seung-hwan   Mike

Changes _____   _____   _____
        _____   _____   _____

Reasons _____   _____   _____
        _____   _____   _____

B. Work with another pair. Take turns explaining your suggestions and your reasons for them. Use this conversation to start but replace the highlighted parts with your own information. How many of your changes are the same? How many are different?

A: *What do you think Mitsuki should do?*
B: *If you ask me, she needs a new haircut. Her hair is too long. And to be honest, she should get some new clothes. They seem like they're really old.*

Lesson 1 Do you like sports?

1 BEFORE YOU LISTEN

A. Are these sports popular in your country? Check (✓) the correct column.

	Popular	Somewhat popular	Not popular
1. hockey	☐	☐	☐
2. skiing	☐	☐	☐
3. golf	☐	☐	☐
4. tennis	☐	☐	☐
5. baseball	☐	☐	☐
6. yoga	☐	☐	☐
7. surfing	☐	☐	☐
8. cycling	☐	☐	☐
9. table tennis	☐	☐	☐
10. badminton	☐	☐	☐
11. volleyball	☐	☐	☐
12. soccer	☐	☐	☐

B. How many of the sports in part A do you enjoy? Circle the sports. Then compare your answers with a partner.

2 LISTEN AND UNDERSTAND 🎧 CD 2 Track 11

A. People are answering a survey at a mall. What do they say about sports and exercise? Listen and circle the correct statement.

1. **a.** She plays tennis every day.   **b.** She prefers playing singles.
2. **a.** He plays basketball once a week.   **b.** He used to belong to an aerobics class.
3. **a.** He enjoys going to the gym.   **b.** He plays volleyball two times a week.
4. **a.** She plays some sports.   **b.** She often goes walking or cycling.
5. **a.** She sometimes goes to the gym.   **b.** She wants to lose weight.

B. Listen again. Is a student or a parent talking in each conversation? Check (✓) the correct column.

	Student	Parent
1.	☐	☐
2.	☐	☐
3.	☐	☐
4.	☐	☐
5.	☐	☐

③ LISTEN AND UNDERSTAND 🎧 CD 2 Track 12

A. Friends are talking about sports events on TV. Did both friends watch the event or only one? Listen and ⟨circle⟩ the correct answer.

1. **a.** both   **b.** only one
2. **a.** both   **b.** only one
3. **a.** both   **b.** only one
4. **a.** both   **b.** only one
5. **a.** both   **b.** only one

B. Listen again. Did they think the sports event was exciting or unexciting? Check (✓) the correct column.

	Exciting	Unexciting
1.	☐	☐
2.	☐	☐
3.	☐	☐
4.	☐	☐
5.	☐	☐

④ TUNE IN 🎧 CD 2 Tracks 13 & 14

A. Listen and notice how people use double questions.

Opening question	+	Focus question
Do you play a lot of sports?	+	***How often do you play?***
How do you keep fit?	+	***Do you play any sports?***
What was the game like?	+	***Who won?***

B. Now match each opening question with its focus question. Then listen and check your answers.

Opening question

1. Do you like winter sports? ___
2. How do you keep fit? ___
3. How often do you go to the gym? ___
4. What sports are popular in your country? ___
5. What sports do you watch on TV? ___

Focus question

a. Is baseball popular?
b. Do you watch soccer?
c. Do you go every day?
d. Have you tried skiing?
e. Do you take exercise classes?

5 **AFTER YOU LISTEN**

A. What do you think about sports? Complete this survey for yourself.

	Me	My partner
1. How do you keep fit?	_____	_____
2. What sports do you play?	_____	_____
3. What sports do you watch?	_____	_____
4. Do your friends play sports?	_____	_____
5. What sports would you like to learn?	_____	_____
6. Does your family like sports?	_____	_____

B. Write focus questions for the questions in part A. The first one is done for you.

Opening question	Focus question
1. How do you keep fit?	_Do you play any sports?_
2. What sports do you play?	_____
3. What sports do you watch?	_____
4. Do your friends play sports?	_____
5. What sports would you like to learn?	_____
6. Does your family like sports?	_____

C. Work with a partner. Take turns asking and answering double questions and complete the survey for your partner. Use this conversation to start but replace the highlighted parts with your own information.

A: *How do you keep fit? Do you play any sports?*
B: *I go to the gym three times a week.*

D. Work with a different partner. Talk about something interesting you learned about your partner in part C.

LESSON OBJECTIVES
▸ Distinguishing facts and opinions
▸ Understanding advice
▸ Expressing agreement and disagreement

Lesson 2   What do you think of boxing on TV?

1 BEFORE YOU LISTEN

What do you know about these sports celebrities? Match each person with the correct description. Then compare your answers with a partner. What else do you know about them?

1. Ian Thorpe ___
2. Ichiro Suzuki ___
3. Maria Sharapova ___
4. Lance Armstrong ___
5. Michelle Wie ___
6. Yao Ming ___

a. She has won many tennis tournaments.
b. He is the seven-time Tour de France champion.
c. He is one of the tallest basketball players in the NBA.
d. She is a young and famous golfer.
e. He is one of the best hitters in baseball.
f. He has won medals for swimming at the Olympic Games.

2 LISTEN AND UNDERSTAND 🎧 CD 2 Track 15

A. Sports experts are answering questions on a radio show. What are the names of the people who sent the questions? Listen and number the people from 1 to 4. There is one extra person in the list.

a. Max ___   **b.** Daiki ___   **c.** Sporty ___   **d.** Sports-fan ___   **e.** Amy ___

B. Listen again. Do the experts give facts or opinions about the topics? Check (✓) the correct column.

	Facts	Opinions
1. Michelle Wie	☐	☐
2. sports stars' money	☐	☐
3. boxing	☐	☐
4. Ichiro Suzuki	☐	☐

ANSWERS: 1. f, 2. e, 3. a, 4. b, 5. d, 6. c

3 LISTEN AND UNDERSTAND 🎧 CD 2 Track 16

A. A baseball coach is talking about preparing for games. Are these things a player should or should not do before a game? Listen and ⟨circle⟩ the correct answer. The first one is done for you.

1. Players *should* / ⟨*should not*⟩ drink soda before a game.
2. Players *should* / *should not* eat a heavy meal before a game.
3. Players *should* / *should not* talk to themselves before a game.
4. Players *should* / *should not* make plans before a game.
5. Players *should* / *should not* get plenty of sleep before a game.

B. Listen again. Fix the mistakes in these sentences. The first one is done for you.

1. Drink plenty of ~~milk~~ before a game. <u>water</u>
2. Eat some nuts before a game. _____
3. The vitamins in fruit can give you energy. _____
4. Talk over your plans with your coach. _____

4 TUNE IN 🎧 CD 2 Tracks 17 & 18

A. Listen and notice how people express agreement and disagreement with an opinion.

Sports celebrities should get paid a lot of money.	
Agreement	**Disagreement**
Definitely. *They work hard.*	*I don't agree.* *It's ridiculous.*
Absolutely. *All celebrities are rich.*	*I don't think so.* *Doctors should get more.*
That's for sure.	*I'm not sure about that.*

B. Now listen to other conversations. Does the person express agreement or disagreement in each conversation? Check (✓) the correct column.

	Agreement	Disagreement
1.	☐	☐
2.	☐	☐
3.	☐	☐
4.	☐	☐
5.	☐	☐
6.	☐	☐

5 AFTER YOU LISTEN

A. Do you agree or disagree with these sports opinions? Complete this survey for yourself.
Check (✓) your opinions.

 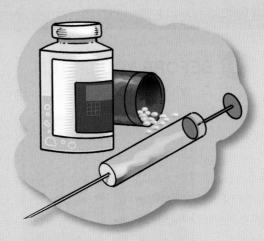

	Me		My partner	
	Agree	Disagree	Agree	Disagree
1. Boxing is a dangerous sport. It should be banned.	☐	☐	☐	☐
2. Young athletes should be 18 years old before turning professional.	☐	☐	☐	☐
3. Athletes who take drugs should be banned for life.	☐	☐	☐	☐
4. There should be more time spent on sports in high school.	☐	☐	☐	☐

B. Why did you agree or disagree? Match each opinion in part A with two of these reasons.
The first one is done for you. Then circle the reasons you agree with.

a. Boxing can lead to serious injury. __1__

b. Playing professional sports is very stressful. ____

c. Students should spend more time studying. ____

d. They are no longer good role models. ____

e. Young athletes are playing like professionals and should be paid like them. ____

f. Sometimes athletes take drugs by mistake. ____

g. There are many other dangerous sports, like ice hockey. ____

h. Young people do not get enough exercise these days. ____

C. Work with a partner. Take turns asking about and answering the opinions in part A and
complete the survey for your partner. Use this conversation to start but replace the
highlighted parts with your own reasons. How many of your reasons are the same?

A: *Do you think boxing is a dangerous sport and should be banned?*
B: *Definitely. Boxing can lead to serious injury.*

The Home

LESSON OBJECTIVES
▸ Making inferences from key words
▸ Identifying housing preferences
▸ Showing interest

Lesson 1 Where do you live?

1 BEFORE YOU LISTEN

A. What kind of home do you live in? Circle the home.

a. apartment   **b.** house   **c.** school dorm

B. Match these features with the correct statements. Then compare your answers with a partner.

1. location ___ ___	**a.** It is near the train station.	**f.** It is just the right price.
2. size ___ ___	**b.** It is too small.	**g.** It is busy and loud.
3. condition ___ ___	**c.** It is newly painted.	**h.** There are good cafes.
4. neighborhood ___ ___	**d.** The furniture does not fit.	**i.** It is far from my school.
5. cost ___ ___	**e.** The stove does not work.	**j.** It is too expensive.

2 LISTEN AND UNDERSTAND 🎧 CD 2 Track 19

A. People are describing homes to friends. What kind of person is talking? Listen and number the people from 1 to 5. There is one extra person in the list.

a. Someone who is moving to a school dorm. ___

b. Someone who wants to rent an apartment. ___

c. Someone who is describing their neighborhood. ___

d. Someone who is describing their house. ___

e. Someone who is talking about their kitchen. ___

f. Someone who is reading an advertisement. ___

B. Listen again. What is the problem with each home? Circle the correct problem.

1.	**a.** It needs some repairs.	**b.** It is far from the bus stop.
2.	**a.** It is too expensive.	**b.** It needs to be painted.
3.	**a.** The bathroom is old.	**b.** The kitchen is too small.
4.	**a.** It is far from the city.	**b.** The neighborhood is loud.
5.	**a.** It is far from the office.	**b.** It is too big.

3 LISTEN AND UNDERSTAND 🎧 CD 2 Tracks 20 & 21

A. Ken is talking to a university housing officer. What kind of housing is he looking for? Listen and check (✓) the correct answer.

1. **location**
   a. near the university ___
   b. not important ___

2. **cost**
   a. under $600 ___
   b. over $600 ___

3. **roommates**
   a. with roommates ___
   b. without roommates ___

4. **facilities**
   a. with kitchen, laundry ___
   b. not important ___

B. Listen to the rest of the conversations. The housing officer is describing different places. Do the places have what Ken is looking for? Check (✓) if the places have the features that are good for Ken. Then circle the best place for Ken.

	Location	Cost	Roommates	Facilities
1.	☐	☐	☐	☐
2.	☐	☐	☐	☐
3.	☐	☐	☐	☐

4 TUNE IN 🎧 CD 2 Tracks 22 & 23

A. Listen and notice how people show interest by asking reply questions.

> **We use rising intonation when we ask reply questions.**
>
> A: *It's very small.*   B: *It is?*
>
> A: *It's quite a nice area to live in. I really like it.*   B: *You do?*
>
> A: *It takes me two hours to get into work.*   B: *It does?*
>
> A: *There is a laundry just down the street.*   B: *There is?*
>
> A: *My sister lives near me.*   B: *She does?*
>
> A: *My roommates are really loud.*   B: *They are?*

B. Now listen to other conversations and circle the reply question you hear.

1. **a.** There is?   **b.** There are?
2. **a.** They did?   **b.** They are?
3. **a.** She does?   **b.** He does?
4. **a.** It is?   **b.** It does?
5. **a.** She does?   **b.** You do?
6. **a.** You do?   **b.** It does?

A. What is your home like? Complete this survey for yourself.

	Me	My partner
1. What kind of home do you live in?	_____	_____
2. Is it big, medium-sized, or small?	_____	_____
3. How many rooms does it have?	_____	_____
4. Who do you live with?	_____	_____
5. What kind of condition is it in?	_____	_____
6. How close is your home to your school?	_____	_____
7. What kind of public transportation is close to your home?	_____	_____
8. What kinds of stores are in your neighborhood?	_____	_____
9. What kinds of restaurants are in your neighborhood?	_____	_____
10. What can you do for fun in your neighborhood?	_____	_____

B. Work with a partner. Take turns asking and answering the questions and complete the survey for your partner. Use this conversation to start but replace the highlighted parts with your own information.

A: *What kind of home do you live in?*
B: *I live in an apartment.*
A: *You do? Is it big, medium-sized, or small?*
B: *It's small.*
A: *It is? How many rooms does it have?*

C. What do you like most about your home and your neighborhood? Tell your partner.

LESSON OBJECTIVES

▸ Identifying features of homes
▸ Identifying topics about homes
▸ Expressing enthusiasm

Lesson 2 What a fantastic home!

① BEFORE YOU LISTEN

What do you think of these unusual homes? Choose a statement in the box for each home. Then compare your answers with a partner.

> It looks weird.   It looks exciting.   It would be my dream home.
> It looks too small.   It looks uncomfortable.   It looks too big for me.

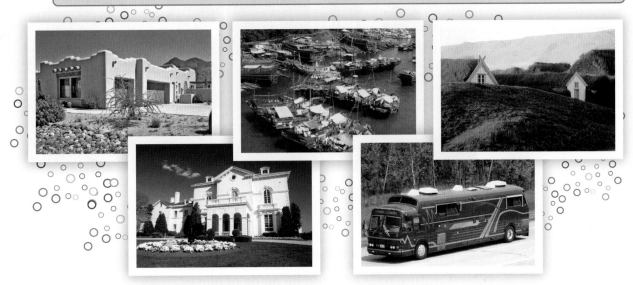

② LISTEN AND UNDERSTAND 🎧 CD 2 Track 24

A. A magazine reporter is interviewing people about their homes. Which features of their homes do they talk about? Listen and check (✓) the correct features. More than one answer is possible.

1. **a.** rooms ___   **b.** cost ___   **c.** comfort ___
2. **a.** length ___   **b.** color ___   **c.** cost ___
3. **a.** building method ___   **b.** neighborhood ___   **c.** comfort ___

B. Listen again. Are these statements true or false? Write *T* (true) or *F* (false).

1. **a.** Jia-hong does not like living in a houseboat. ___
   b. The houseboat is too small for the family. ___
   c. The family does not often move the boat. ___

2. **a.** There are many different rooms in the trailer. ___
   b. The home is convenient because the family moves often. ___
   c. The family is planning to go to New York next month. ___

3. **a.** Susan lives in an apartment building. ___
   b. The house is very dark. ___
   c. The sunlight helps them save energy. ___

③ LISTEN AND UNDERSTAND 🎧 CD 2 Track 25

A. A radio show host is talking to an architect about future homes. Which topics do they talk about? Listen and circle the correct topics. More than one answer is possible.

a. building locations   **c.** neighborhoods   **e.** building costs
b. building materials   **d.** noise   **f.** size

B. Listen again. Are these statements true or false? Write *T* (true) or *F* (false).

1. Future houses could be made of plastic. ___

2. Future houses will have more rooms. ___

3. Future houses may be built in or under the water. ___

4. Future houses will be built by computers. ___

④ TUNE IN 🎧 CD 2 Tracks 26 & 27

A. Listen and notice how people express enthusiasm.

A: *We live on a houseboat.*	**B:** *That sounds cool.*
A: *The trailer is 30 meters long.*	**B:** *That's amazing!*
A: *The house gets a lot of sunlight and saves energy.*	**B:** *That's terrific.*
A: *In the future, we may live in underwater homes.*	**B:** *That's incredible!*

B. Now listen to a conversation and number the expressions you hear from 1 to 4.

a. That's amazing! ___

b. That's terrific. ___

c. That's incredible! ___

d. That sounds cool. ___

5 AFTER YOU LISTEN

A. What kind of home would you like to live in? Complete this survey for yourself. Check (✓) your preferences and add your own options for each section.

PLAN YOUR IDEAL HOME

1. What kind of home will it be?

house ☐
apartment ☐
houseboat ☐
trailer ☑
underground home ☐
castle ☐
_____

3. Where will it be?

downtown ☐
in the suburbs ☐
in the countryside ☑
by the beach ☐
in the mountains ☐
in the desert ☐
_____

2. How many rooms will it have? Write the number.

kitchen _____
living room _____
family room _____
bedroom _____
bathroom _____
garage _____
_____
_____

4. What special facilities will it have?

home movie theater ☐
gym ☐
sauna ☐
indoor pool ☐
outdoor pool ☐
yard ☐
tennis court ☐
_____
_____

B. Work with a partner. Compare your answers. Use this conversation to start but replace the highlighted parts with your own information. How many of your features are the same?

A: *What kind of home will it be?*

B: *It'll be an apartment.*

A: *Where will it be?*

B: *It'll be downtown and by the river.*

A: *That sounds cool. How many rooms will it have?*

B: *It'll have four bedrooms, two bathrooms, a huge kitchen, and a living room.*

A: *Wow! What special facilities will it have?*

B: *It'll have a gym, a sauna, and a home movie theater.*

A: *That's amazing!*

LESSON OBJECTIVES
▸ Identifying sequences of events
▸ Understanding descriptions of jobs
▸ Checking understanding

Lesson 1   What an amazing animal!

1 **BEFORE YOU LISTEN**

A. What are these animals like? Choose adjectives in the box that describe each animal. Then compare your answers with a partner.

loyal	brave	curious	independent
cautious	affectionate	intelligent	noisy

Dog _____   **Cat** _____   **Chimpanzee** _____   **Parrot** _____

B. Work with a partner. Choose an adjective in part A to complete these newspaper headlines.

_____ **Cat Finds Its Way Home**

_____ **Dog Cares for Baby**

_____ **Parrot Saves Children from Fire**

_____ **Chimpanzee Paints Pictures**

2 **LISTEN AND UNDERSTAND** 🎧 CD 2 Track 28

A. People are calling a radio show to tell amazing true stories about animals. Listen and number the story events in the correct order.

Story 1

___ They came back from their vacation.

___ The cat escaped from the house.

___ They saw the cat's name on the tag.

___ A family went overseas for vacation.

___ They heard a cat in the yard.

Story 2

___ A dog found the baby.

___ The dog became a hero.

___ Someone heard the baby crying.

___ The dog cared for the baby.

___ Someone left a baby in a parking lot.

B. Listen again. Are these statements true or false? Write *T* (true) or *F* (false).

Story 1
a. The story happened in Australia. ___
b. The grandparents lived nearby. ___
c. The cat was healthy when it returned. ___

Story 2
a. The dog was wild. ___
b. The baby was hurt. ___
c. A family took the baby. ___

3 LISTEN AND UNDERSTAND 🎧 CD 2 Track 29

A. People are talking to dog owners about their dogs. What do the dogs do? Listen and number the dogs from 1 to 4.

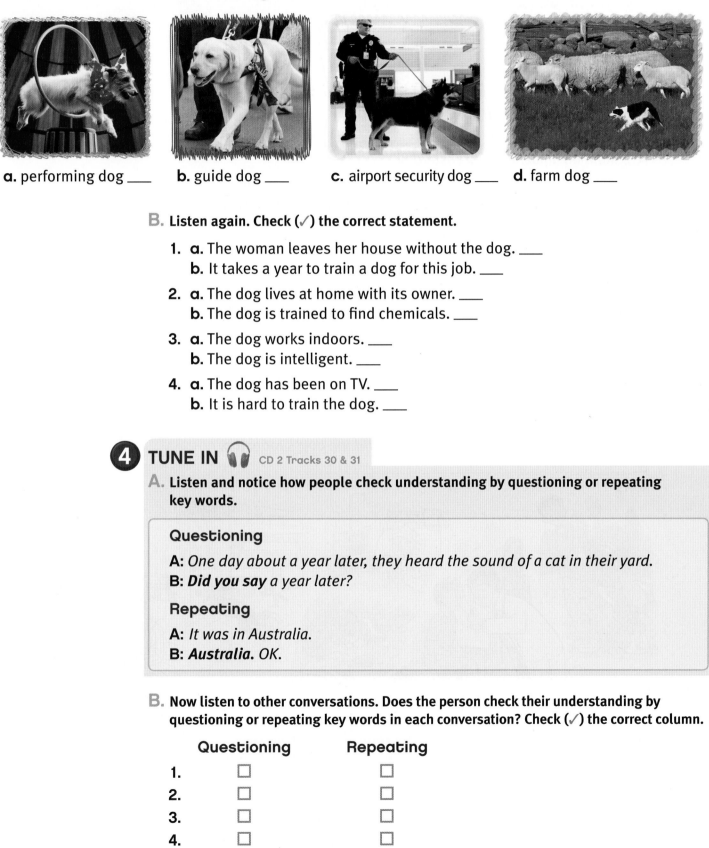

a. performing dog ___   **b.** guide dog ___   **c.** airport security dog ___   **d.** farm dog ___

B. Listen again. Check (✓) the correct statement.

1. **a.** The woman leaves her house without the dog. ___
   b. It takes a year to train a dog for this job. ___

2. **a.** The dog lives at home with its owner. ___
   b. The dog is trained to find chemicals. ___

3. **a.** The dog works indoors. ___
   b. The dog is intelligent. ___

4. **a.** The dog has been on TV. ___
   b. It is hard to train the dog. ___

4 TUNE IN 🎧 CD 2 Tracks 30 & 31

A. Listen and notice how people check understanding by questioning or repeating key words.

> **Questioning**
>
> **A:** *One day about a year later, they heard the sound of a cat in their yard.*
> **B:** ***Did you say*** *a year later?*
>
> **Repeating**
>
> **A:** *It was in Australia.*
> **B:** ***Australia.*** *OK.*

B. Now listen to other conversations. Does the person check their understanding by questioning or repeating key words in each conversation? Check (✓) the correct column.

	Questioning	Repeating
1.	☐	☐
2.	☐	☐
3.	☐	☐
4.	☐	☐
5.	☐	☐

⑤ AFTER YOU LISTEN

A. Work with a partner. Choose sentences in the box to complete the conversation.

> Did you say disappeared? Where did it go?
> An operation. Oh, no!
> Did you say a hospital?
> You did? What was it about?
> A window. Wow. But how did the dog find the hospital?
> Was the dog allowed to stay?

A: *I heard an amazing story yesterday.*

B: _____

A: *Well, it was about a dog that got into a hospital to visit a sick boy.*

B: _____

A: *Yeah. Apparently, the boy was the dog's owner and he got really sick. He had to have an operation.*

B: _____

A: *I know. Poor kid. But while the boy was away, the dog became really sad and wouldn't eat. Then one day it disappeared.*

B: _____

A: *Well, it found the boy's hospital and jumped through a window.*

B: _____

A: *It was in the car when the parents took the boy to the hospital. The dog remembered where it was and then found the boy's room too.*

B: _____

B. Choose the best ending in the box for the story or think of your own.

> The dog only stayed one day.   The parents needed the dog at home.
> The dog was allowed to stay until the boy got well.   The doctors took the dog away.

C. Work with a partner. Practice the conversation in part A with your partner. Add the ending that you chose in part B.

LESSON OBJECTIVES
▸ Understanding descriptions of animals
▸ Identifying topics about animals
▸ Responding to surprising news

Lesson 2 I didn't know animals could do that

1 BEFORE YOU LISTEN

What do you know about these animals? Match each animal with the correct fact. Then compare your answers with a partner. Do you know anything more about these animals?

a. koala

b. komodo dragon

c. ostrich

d. cheetah

e. bat

f. penguin

1. This animal has special eyes and can see clearly under water. ____
2. There are nearly 1,000 species of this animal. ____
3. This is the fastest land animal. It can run over 100 kilometers per hour. ____
4. This animal has saliva that is deadly and poisonous. ____
5. This is the largest bird. It can reach a height of three meters. ____
6. This animal has two thumbs. ____

2 LISTEN AND UNDERSTAND 🎧 CD 2 Track 32

A. **A zookeeper is describing different animals to children. Listen and number the animals from 1 to 4.**

a. komodo dragon ____   **b.** koala ____   **c.** penguin ____   **d.** bat ____

B. **Listen again. Check (✓) the statements that are true for each animal.**

	Penguin	Bat	Koala	Komodo dragon
1. active at night	☐	☐	☐	☐
2. sleeps a lot	☐	☐	☐	☐
3. can weigh more than 150 kilograms	☐	☐	☐	☐
4. eats snakes	☐	☐	☐	☐
5. eats fish	☐	☐	☐	☐
6. lives for about 20 years	☐	☐	☐	☐

ANSWERS: 1. f, 2. e, 3. d, 4. b, 5. c, 6. a

3 LISTEN AND UNDERSTAND 🎧 CD 2 Track 33

A. Visitors at a zoo are listening to recorded information about polar bears. Which topics do they hear? Listen and check (✓) the correct topics. More than one answer is possible.

a. diet ___   **c.** weight ___   **e.** enemies ___

b. cubs ___   **d.** intelligence ___   **f.** bodies ___

B. Listen again. Are these statements true or false? Write *T* (true) or *F* (false).

1. Male and female bears are the same size. ___
2. The bears are found in five different countries. ___
3. The cubs drink milk for more than two years. ___
4. Male bears sometimes kill the cubs. ___
5. The bears have a layer of fat that is six centimeters thick. ___

4 TUNE IN 🎧 CD 2 Tracks 34 & 35

A. Listen and notice how people respond to surprising news.

> **A:** *That's all they ever eat—just fish.*   **B:** *That's weird.*
>
> **A:** *They spend 75 percent of their lives at sea.*   **B:** *That's hard to believe.*
>
> **A:** *They don't have any feathers on their wings.*   **B:** *I didn't know that.*
>
> **A:** *Some of them live up to 40 years.*   **B:** *That's incredible!*
>
> **A:** *They can weigh more than 150 kilograms.*   **B:** *That's amazing!*
>
> **A:** *They can even eat each other.*   **B:** *Unbelievable!*

B. Now listen to other conversations and number the expressions you hear from 1 to 6.

a. That's weird. ___

b. I didn't know that. ___

c. Unbelievable! ___

d. That's incredible! ___

e. That's amazing! ___

f. That's hard to believe. ___

5 AFTER YOU LISTEN

A. How much do you know about animals? Read the statements in the Amazing Animals Quiz. Check (✓) the statements that are true.

Amazing Animals

		Me	My partner
1	Hippopotamuses give birth under water.	☐	☐
2	Cows produce about 33,600 glasses of milk per year.	☐	☐
3	Baby blue whales weigh about five tons at birth.	☐	☐
4	Elephants carry their young for 22 months before giving birth.	☐	☐
5	Dolphins sleep with one eye open.	☐	☐
6	Cats see six times better at night than humans.	☐	☐
7	Monkeys often eat their own young.	☐	☐
8	An ostrich's eye is bigger than its brain.	☐	☐
9	Ants never sleep.	☐	☐
10	Penguins can go for over 100 days withour food.	☐	☐
11	Polar bears are left-handed.	☐	☐
12	Goldfish live to be about 50 years old.	☐	☐

B. Work with a partner. Take turns asking about the statements and answering them. Complete the quiz for your partner. Use this conversation to start but replace the highlighted parts with your own answers.

A: *"Hippopotamuses give birth under water." That's weird. Do you think it's true or false?*

B: *I think it's false. What do you think?*

A: *I think it's true.*

C. Check your answers below. How many did you get correct?

Answers: 1, 2, 4, 5, 6, 8, 10, 11 are true

LESSON OBJECTIVES
▸ Identifying free time activities
▸ Describing likes and dislikes
▸ Accepting and declining invitations

Lesson 1   How do you spend your free time?

1 BEFORE YOU LISTEN

What do you do in your free time? Circle activities in the box and add two more of your own. Then compare your answers with a partner.

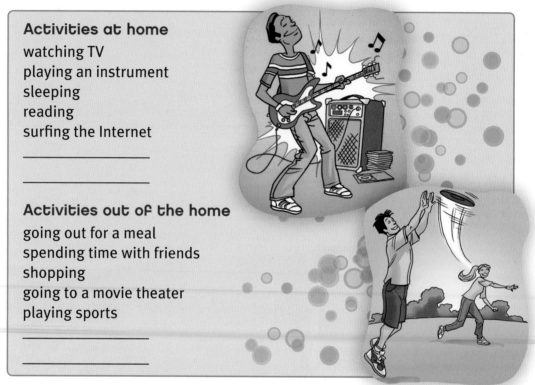

Activities at home
watching TV
playing an instrument
sleeping
reading
surfing the Internet

_____

_____

Activities out of the home
going out for a meal
spending time with friends
shopping
going to a movie theater
playing sports

_____

_____

2 LISTEN AND UNDERSTAND 🎧 CD 2 Track 36

A. Friends are doing activities in their free time. Listen and number the activities from 1 to 5.

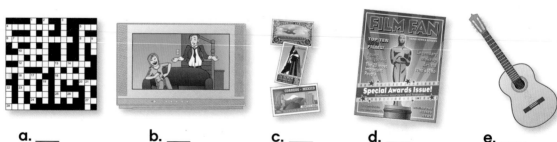

a. ___   b. ___   c. ___   d. ___   e. ___

B. Listen again. Are these statements true or false? Write *T* (true) or *F* (false).

1. The friends live in Mexico. ___
2. The friend loves to hear him play. ___
3. The correct answer is *good*. ___
4. The friends are watching a movie. ___
5. The friends are at home. ___

3 LISTEN AND UNDERSTAND 🎧 CD 2 Track 37

A. People are making suggestions about what to do on a cold Sunday afternoon. Do their friends like or dislike the suggested activity? Listen and check (✓) the correct column.

	Like	Dislike
1. reading comic books	☐	☐
2. watching a cartoon show	☐	☐
3. playing a racing game	☐	☐
4. playing a card game	☐	☐
5. listening to heavy metal music	☐	☐

B. Listen again. What will happen next? Circle the best answer.

1. **a.** Dan will read magazines.
   b. Dan and Peter will go out.
2. **a.** Kazu and Mike will keep watching the show.
   b. Kazu will switch channels.
3. **a.** Mei-ling and Seon-hee will listen to some music.
   b. Mei-ling and Seon-hee will play a sports game.
4. **a.** James will show Andrew how to play the game.
   b. Andrew will suggest something different to do.
5. **a.** Carla and Martin will play some music.
   b. Carla and Martin will look for a magazine.

4 TUNE IN 🎧 CD 2 Tracks 38 & 39

A. Listen and notice how people accept and decline invitations.

Invitations	Accept
What about some magazines?	*That would be great.*
How about a sports game?	*That sounds great.*
Do you want to play a card game?	*Thanks. I'd love to.*
	Decline
Do you want to help me solve this?	*I'd love to, but you know I'm hopeless.*
Do you want to take a look?	*Sorry, but I'm not really into comics.*
Do you want to try the game?	*I'm afraid I can't stand racing games.*

B. Now listen to other conversations. Does the person accept or decline the invitation in each conversation? Check (✓) the correct column.

	Accept	Decline
1.	☐	☐
2.	☐	☐
3.	☐	☐
4.	☐	☐
5.	☐	☐

5 **AFTER YOU LISTEN**

A. **Match each invitation with the correct response. Then practice the conversations with a partner.**

1. Would you like to see that new Angelina Jolie movie? ___
2. How about coming over and playing computer games? ___
3. Why don't we go to the jazz club on Friday night? ___
4. Do you feel like going for a bike ride on Sunday? ___
5. Do you want to check out the sales at the mall this weekend? ___

a. Sorry, but I have a cold and I need to stay indoors.
b. That sounds great. I love jazz!
c. I'd love to, but I'm broke! I have to start saving money.
d. Thanks. I'd love to. She's my favorite actress.
e. That would be great. I'll bring some of my own games too.

B. **What activities do you want to do this weekend? Make a list.**

1. _____

2. _____

3. _____

4. _____

C. **Work with a partner. Take turns inviting your partner to do the activities in part B. Accept some invitations and decline some invitations. When you decline, use excuses in the box or think of your own excuses.**

I have to take my dog for a walk.	I have a yoga lesson.
I have an appointment with my dentist.	I have to babysit my cousins.

LESSON OBJECTIVES
▸ Making inferences from key words
▸ Understanding descriptions of hobbies
▸ Making assumptions

Lesson 2 That's an unusual hobby

1 BEFORE YOU LISTEN

What do you think of these hobbies? Rank this list from 1 (most interesting) to 11 (least interesting). Then compare your answers with a partner.

___ collecting soda cans

___ designing clothes

___ writing poetry

___ collecting movie posters

___ computer programming

___ running

___ doing jigsaw puzzles

___ playing online computer games

___ painting

___ taking photos

___ surfing

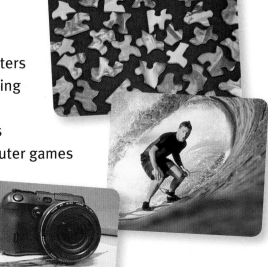

2 LISTEN AND UNDERSTAND 🎧 CD 2 Track 40

A. **People are talking about their hobbies. Listen and number the hobbies from 1 to 4. There is one extra hobby in the list.**

a. designing clothes ___

b. collecting soda cans ___

c. writing poetry ___

d. playing online computer games ___

e. running ___

B. **Listen again. Check (✓) the correct statement.**

1.
a. She just started doing it. ___
b. She makes friends this way. ___
c. She only plays a little. ___

2.
a. She got her first one while traveling. ___
b. She does not have many yet. ___
c. She gets them from his parents. ___

3.
a. It is a good summer activity. ___
b. It is a good activity for the brain. ___
c. He has not published any. ___

4.
a. He does it every day. ___
b. None of his friends do it. ___
c. He gets new shoes often. ___

3 LISTEN AND UNDERSTAND 🎧 CD 2 Track 41

A. A radio show host is interviewing people about things they collect. Listen and check (✓) the correct statement.

1. a. Yuko just started collecting phone cards. ___
   b. Yuko has cards worth more than $50. ___

2. a. Jacob has been collecting photos for about three years. ___
   b. Photos usually cost more than $100. ___

3. a. Virginia only collects photos of the Beatles. ___
   b. Virginia started collecting after she visited England. ___

B. Listen again. How did the collectors build their collections? Circle the correct answer.

1. Yuko   **a.** by buying from stores
          b. by buying from the Internet

2. Jacob   **a.** by buying from fan clubs
          b. by ordering from catalogs

3. Virginia **a.** by ordering from fan magazines
          b. by buying from stores

4 TUNE IN 🎧 CD 2 Tracks 42 & 43

A. Listen and notice how people make assumptions.

> A: *You can make friends with people all over the world.*
> B: ***That must** be fun.*
>
> A: *I have over 100 cans.*
> B: ***That sounds** like a great collection.*
>
> A: *The best place to find things is in fan magazines.*
> B: ***I guess** you're a big Beatles fan then.*

B. Now listen to other conversations and circle the expression you hear.

1. **a.** that sounds   **b.** that must
2. **a.** I guess   **b.** that sounds
3. **a.** that must   **b.** I guess
4. **a.** that must   **b.** that sounds
5. **a.** that sounds   **b.** I guess
6. **a.** that must   **b.** that sounds

5 AFTER YOU LISTEN

A. What are your hobbies and interests? Complete this survey for yourself. Add two more activities of your own and check (✓) the things you do.

	Me	My partner
1. surfing the Internet	☐	☐
2. reading books	☐	☐
3. playing an instrument	☐	☐
4. taking photos	☐	☐
5. playing baseball	☐	☐
6. swimming	☐	☐
7. playing soccer	☐	☐
8. playing online computer games	☐	☐
9. listening to music	☐	☐
10. watching movies	☐	☐
11. drawing	☐	☐
12. going shopping	☐	☐
13. _____	☐	☐
14. _____	☐	☐

B. Work with a partner. Take turns telling each other the activities you checked and complete the survey for your partner. Write assumptions about five of your partner's activities.

1. _____
2. _____
3. _____
4. _____
5. _____

C. Work with a partner. Take turns asking and making assumptions about the activities in part B. Use this conversation to start but replace the highlighted parts with your own information.

A: *What do you like to do in your free time?*

B: *I like surfing the Internet.*

A: *I guess you're indoors a lot then.*

Buying Things

Lesson 1 It's a great gift

1 BEFORE YOU LISTEN

A. What gifts would you buy these people for their birthdays? Choose gifts in the box or think of your own. Then compare your answers with a partner.

a vase	a movie	a tie	a gift certificate	perfume
a T-shirt	a camera	a book	a magazine subscription	a scarf

1. father _____
2. mother _____
3. best friend _____
4. grandparents _____
5. young niece _____
6. young nephew _____

B. What gifts did you get for your last birthday? Discuss with a partner.

2 LISTEN AND UNDERSTAND 🎧 CD 3 Track 02

A. Shoppers are talking with sales clerks about gifts. Listen and number the gifts from 1 to 5.

a. ___   b. ___   c. ___   d. ___   e. ___

B. Listen again. Will the customer buy the item? Check (✓) the correct column.

	Yes	No
1.	☐	☐
2.	☐	☐
3.	☐	☐
4.	☐	☐
5.	☐	☐

3 LISTEN AND UNDERSTAND 🎧 CD 3 Track 03

A. Friends are talking about gifts to buy in a store. Which gift will they choose? Listen and circle the correct answer.

1. **a.** the ring
   b. the watch

2. **a.** the CD
   b. the DVD

3. **a.** the vase
   b. the bowl

4. **a.** the sweater
   b. the cap

5. **a.** the perfume
   b. the scarf

B. Listen again. Why did they choose each gift? Check (✓) the correct statement.

1. **a.** It is cheaper. ___   **b.** It is more useful. ___
2. **a.** It is a better price. ___   **b.** He can play it. ___
3. **a.** The color is more suitable. ___   **b.** It is a better shape. ___
4. **a.** He likes the team. ___   **b.** It is more comfortable. ___
5. **a.** She wears it every day. ___   **b.** She prefers the style. ___

4 TUNE IN 🎧 CD 3 Tracks 04 & 05

A. Listen and notice how people buy time to think using echo questions.

> **A:** *You have to walk them two or three times a day.*
> **B:** ***Two or three times a day?*** *Oh, that's not a problem.*
>
> **A:** *It's the latest of this kind.*
> **B:** ***The latest?*** *Really? OK, then.*
>
> **A:** *What about a baseball cap?*
> **B:** ***A baseball cap?*** *Yes, maybe.*

B. Now circle the words a person might echo in each sentence. Then listen and check your answers.

1. I'd like to buy an Art Blakey CD.
2. Can I get things gift wrapped at this store?
3. They're the most popular skis in the store.
4. I'm looking for rice cookers. Do you know where I can find them?
5. This computer is on sale until next Thursday.
6. It'd be perfect for a young child, for example.

5 AFTER YOU LISTEN

A. What gifts can you give on these occasions? Complete this survey for yourself. Choose gifts in the box or think of your own.

a digital camera	flowers	a CD	a gift certificate	a puzzle	a tie
an MP3 player	a watch	a book	a bicycle	a sweater	a toy

	A best friend's college graduation	A cousin's seventh birthday	A classmate's farewell party
Expensive	_____	_____	_____
Somewhat expensive	_____	_____	_____
Cheap	_____	_____	_____

B. Work with a partner. Take turns asking and answering questions about the gifts you chose. Use this conversation to start but replace the highlighted parts with your own information.

A: *What can I buy for a classmate's farewell party? I want to buy a cheap gift.*

B: *A cheap gift? Well, I suppose you could buy some flowers.*

A: *Some flowers? Yeah, that's a good idea.*

C. Work with another pair. Compare your answers. Who had the most unusual gift? Who had the funniest gift?

LESSON OBJECTIVES
▸ Identifying locations in a mall
▸ Identifying features of malls
▸ Confirming information

Lesson 2 Let's meet at the mall

1 BEFORE YOU LISTEN

What do you like to do at the mall? Check (✓) activities in the list and add two more of your own. Then compare your answers with a partner.

1. get a haircut ___
2. hang out with friends ___
3. play arcade games ___
4. go window-shopping ___
5. see a show ___
6. have a meal ___
7. hear live music ___
8. make a bank deposit ___
9. _____
10. _____

2 LISTEN AND UNDERSTAND 🎧 CD 3 Track 06

A. People are at different places in a mall. Where are they? Listen and number the places from 1 to 6. There is one extra place in the list.

a. sports store ___

b. hair salon ___

c. movie theater ___

d. CD store ___

e. flower shop ___

f. bank ___

g. cafe ___

B. Listen again. Are these statements true or false? Write *T* (true) or *F* (false).

1. The man does not buy anything. ___

2. The friends are going to get different things. ___

3. The store has what he is looking for. ___

4. The woman has been there before. ___

5. The man wants to spend $50. ___

6. The goggles come in different sizes. ___

LISTEN AND UNDERSTAND 🎧 CD 3 Track 07

A. Customers are listening to recorded information about malls. Which features are mentioned? Listen and check (✓) the correct column.

	Fairway	Central	Golden	Parklane
1. special prices	☐	☐	☐	☐
2. number of stores	☐	☐	☐	☐
3. location of the mall	☐	☐	☐	☐
4. special attractions for children	☐	☐	☐	☐

B. Listen again. Fix the mistakes in these notes.

> Fairway Mall
> open Monday to Friday 10-6,
> Saturday to Sunday 10-9
> live music Saturday/Sunday morning
> clowns Sunday morning

1. _____

> Golden Mall
> open 9-6 all week
> City Tigers signing autographs on Monday
> one cash prize of $5,000 every day

3. _____

> Central Mall
> open Monday to Friday 9-6,
> Saturday to Sunday 9-9
> 20% discount in all stores
> cinemas $1 all day Sunday

2. _____

> Parklane Mall
> open Monday to Friday 10-5,
> Saturday to Sunday 10-7
> International Food Festival
> free cooking lessons every day

4. _____

4 **TUNE IN** 🎧 CD 3 Tracks 08 & 09

A. Listen and notice how people confirm information by using tag questions.

> The movie is at 2:30, **isn't it?**
> The sandwiches are really good here, **aren't they?**
> You usually like your hair quite long, **don't you?**
> There are a lot to choose from, **aren't there?**
> These goggles don't come in different sizes, **do they?**

B. Now circle the correct tag question for each sentence. Then listen and check your answers.

1. The mall closes at 9 P.M.,	**a.** doesn't it?	**b.** does it?
2. You sell tennis racquets here,	**a.** don't they?	**b.** don't you?
3. The elevators are over there,	**a.** is it?	**b.** aren't they?
4. You don't open on Sundays,	**a.** do you?	**b.** are you?
5. There's plenty of parking at the mall,	**a.** isn't there?	**b.** is there?
6. The new mall isn't far,	**a.** is it?	**b.** isn't it?

5 AFTER YOU LISTEN

A. Complete each sentence with its correct tag question. Add two more questions of your own. Then complete this survey for yourself.

	Me Yes	Me No	My partner Yes	My partner No
1. You go shopping every week, _____?	☐	☐	☐	☐
2. Malls don't have good sales on weekdays, _____?	☐	☐	☐	☐
3. There are great deals on video games at the moment, _____?	☐	☐	☐	☐
4. You buy all your clothes at malls, _____?	☐	☐	☐	☐
5. The most modern movie theaters are in malls, _____?	☐	☐	☐	☐
6. The best place to buy music is in malls, _____?	☐	☐	☐	☐
7. Shopping is easier to do in a mall, _____?	☐	☐	☐	☐
8. Malls don't have good restaurants, _____?	☐	☐	☐	☐
9. January is the best month for sales, _____?	☐	☐	☐	☐
10. Malls are the best places to meet friends, _____?	☐	☐	☐	☐
11. _____?	☐	☐	☐	☐
12. _____?	☐	☐	☐	☐

B. Work with a partner. Take turns asking and answering the questions and complete the survey for your partner. Use this conversation to start but replace the highlighted parts with your own information.

A: *You go shopping every week, don't you?*
B: *Yes, I do. I usually go Saturday and Sunday. I love shopping.*

B: *Malls don't have good sales on weekdays, do they?*
A: *Actually they do. In fact, they have better sales on weekdays than on weekends.*

Unit 12   Great Inventions

LESSON OBJECTIVES
▶ Understanding descriptions of inventions
▶ Making inferences from key words
▶ Expressing degrees of uncertainty

Lesson 1   When was that invented?

1 BEFORE YOU LISTEN

What do you know about these items? Circle the correct date for each statement. Then check your answers below. How many did you get correct?

	a.	b.
1. Blue jeans were first made in	a. 1948	b. 1873
2. Skateboards were first sold in	a. 1959	b. 1989
3. Soft contact lenses were developed in the	a. 1890s	b. 1970s
4. Scotch tape was invented in	a. 1930	b. 1780
5. Microwave ovens were developed in	a. 1815	b. 1954
6. Personal computers were first sold in the	a. 1940s	b. 1970s
7. CDs were first produced in	a. 1922	b. 1983
8. Cell phones were first sold in the	a. 1980s	b. 1960s
9. Coca-cola was first made in	a. 1886	b. 1704
10. The World Wide Web was developed in	a. 1970	b. 1990

2 LISTEN AND UNDERSTAND 🎧 CD 3 Track 10

A. A museum has recorded information about its exhibits. Listen and circle the correct answer.

1. camera
  a. George Eastman introduced his box camera in 1893.
  b. George Eastman was American.

2. DVD
  a. It was first developed in 1995.
  b. The inventors wanted something small.

3. Razor scooter
  a. It took five years to develop.
  b. It was only popular in Asia.

4. windshield wipers
  a. They were invented in Europe.
  b. They were first made for streetcars.

B. Listen again. Check (✓) the statements that are true for each invention.

	Camera	DVD	Razor scooter	Windshield wipers
1. was invented before 1950	☐	☐	☐	☐
2. was invented by a woman	☐	☐	☐	☐
3. was invented in Asia	☐	☐	☐	☐

ANSWERS: 1. b, 2. a, 3. b, 4. a, 5. b, 6. b, 7. b, 8. a, 9. a, 10. b

3 LISTEN AND UNDERSTAND 🎧 CD 3 Track 11

A. A teacher is talking to a class. Listen and check (✓) the correct answers.

1. Which one of these courses is the class taking?
   a. History of the Media: Television in the 20th Century ___
   b. Basic Electronics: Understanding and Repairing Televisions ___
   c. Popular Culture: The Influence of Television ___
   d. Electronics and Design: The Changing Shape of Televisions ___

2. Which three topics does the teacher talk about?
   a. the man who first developed TV ___
   b. when color TV was first developed ___
   c. why cable TV was developed ___
   d. why plasma TVs were developed ___

B. Listen again. Fix the mistakes in the sentences.

1. The first demonstration of TV was in 1933. _____
2. Color TV was first developed in 1950. _____
3. Cable TV was developed in 1968. _____
4. Plasma TVs started appearing in the 1980s. _____

4 TUNE IN 🎧 CD 3 Tracks 12 & 13

A. Listen and notice how people express degrees of uncertainty.

A: *When do you think TV was invented?*	**B:** *I think it was around 1960.* **B:** *I guess it was some time in the 1960s.* **B:** *It was probably around 1980.* **B:** *It must have been in the 90s.*	**Less certain** ↓ **More certain**

B. Now listen to other conversations. Check (✓) these expressions each time you hear them.

1. I think   ___ ___ ___ ___
2. I guess   ___ ___ ___ ___
3. It was probably ___ ___ ___ ___
4. It must have been ___ ___ ___ ___

A. When were these common items invented? Complete this quiz. Circle the correct answers.

WHEN WERE THESE THINGS INVENTED?

		a.	b.	c.
1.	zippers	a. 1913	b. 1934	c. 1951
2.	batteries	a. 1780	b. 1800	c. 1900
3.	laptop computers	a. 1964	b. 1972	c. 1983
4.	Post-it notes	a. 1974	b. 1989	c. 1993
5.	basketball	a. 1790	b. 1891	c. 1969
6.	air conditioners	a. 1902	b. 1922	c. 1941
7.	airplanes	a. 1903	b. 1917	c. 1948
8.	photocopiers	a. 1895	b. 1903	c. 1937
9.	e-mail	a. 1964	b. 1971	c. 1989
10.	potato chips	a. 1853	b. 1899	c. 1911

B. Work with a partner. Take turns asking and answering questions about the items and compare your answers. Use these conversations to start but replace the highlighted parts with your own information. Then check your answers below. How many did you get correct?

A: *When do you think zippers were invented?*
B: *It must have been in 1913. What do you think?*
A: *Yes, I agree.*

B: *When do you think batteries were invented?*
A: *It was probably in 1900. What do you think?*
B: *I don't think so. I think it was in 1800.*

ANSWERS: 1.a, 2.b, 3.c, 4.a, 5.b, 6.a, 7.a, 8.c, 9.b, 10.a

LESSON OBJECTIVES

▸ Identifying items from descriptions
▸ Making inferences from context
▸ Checking understanding

Lesson 2 I'd love to get one of those

1 BEFORE YOU LISTEN

A. What do you think these unusual products are for? Match each product with the correct use. Then compare your answers with a partner.

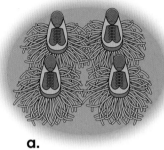
a.

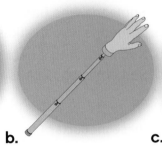
b.

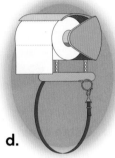
c.

d.

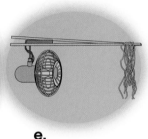
e.

1. to wear in the office ____
2. to wear when you have a cold or allergies ____
3. to cool hot noodles when you eat ____
4. to put on a pet so it can clean things ____
5. to reach things far away ____

B. Would you buy any of these items? Discuss with a partner.

2 LISTEN AND UNDERSTAND 🎧 CD 3 Track 14

A. Friends are looking at unusual products. Listen and number the products from 1 to 5. There is one extra product in the list.

a. lazy grabber ____
b. umbrella for shoppers ____
c. subway chin stand ____
d. noodle cooler ____
e. cleaning shoes for pets ____
f. pocket tie ____

B. Listen again. Does the speaker think the unusual product is a good idea or a bad idea? Check (✓) the correct column.

	Good idea	Bad idea
1.	☐	☐
2.	☐	☐
3.	☐	☐
4.	☐	☐
5.	☐	☐

3 LISTEN AND UNDERSTAND CD 3 Track 15

A. A sales clerk is describing store products. What kind of person would buy these products? Listen and (circle) the correct answer.

1. **a.** Someone with a large house.
   b. Someone with a small house.
2. **a.** Someone with a noisy dog.
   b. Someone with a small dog.
3. **a.** Someone who likes baking.
   b. Someone who wants to save money.
4. **a.** Someone who has children.
   b. Someone who dislikes doing housework.
5. **a.** Someone with a backache.
   b. Someone who is busy.

B. Listen again. What are the features of these products? Check (✓) the correct answer.

1. **a.** stores telephone numbers ___   **b.** takes pictures ___
2. **a.** massages the dog ___   **b.** tells you where the dog is ___
3. **a.** makes drinks ___   **b.** takes only 20 minutes ___
4. **a.** plays music ___   **b.** cleans different kinds of floors ___
5. **a.** uses heat ___   **b.** has many different programs ___

4 TUNE IN CD 3 Tracks 16 & 17

A. Listen and notice how people check their understanding.

> **A:** *It's for getting things that are far away.*
> **B:** ***So does that mean*** *if I can't reach something, I use this?*
>
> **A:** *It's got little pockets in the back.*
> **B:** ***So that means*** *you can carry all sorts of things in it.*
>
> **A:** *I think you make it stand, and you rest your chin on it.*
> **B:** ***So I guess*** *you could sleep standing up in the subway.*

B. Now listen to other conversations and (circle) the expression you hear.

1. **a.** So I guess   **b.** So does that mean
2. **a.** So I guess   **b.** So that means
3. **a.** So I guess   **b.** So does that mean
4. **a.** So I guess   **b.** So that means
5. **a.** So I guess   **b.** So does that mean
6. **a.** So I guess   **b.** So that means

5 AFTER YOU LISTEN

A. Match each invention with its sentence that checks understanding. Then practice the conversations with a partner.

1. The subway chin stand is for commuters. ___
2. The umbrella is for shoppers. ___
3. The cooler makes hot noodles cool. ___
4. The slippers are for a pet to clean the floor. ___
5. The grabber helps you reach things. ___

a. So that means you can keep your bags dry.
b. So does that mean you never need to clean?
c. So I guess you won't burn your mouth.
d. So I guess it's good for lazy people.
e. So does that mean you can use it to sleep on the subway?

B. Work with a partner. Match these inventions with a possible use in the boxes or think of a use of your own. Then write when each invention could be used and what kind of person would find it useful.

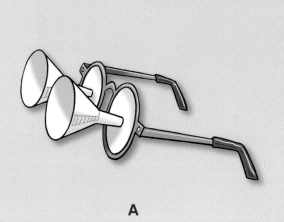

A

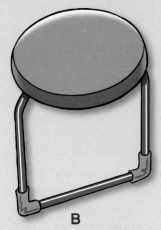

B

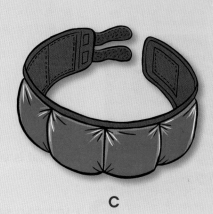

C

eyedrops glasses	a foldable picnic table	a fanny pack
binoculars	a baby's high chair	a head cooler
glasses cleaner	a commuter's chair	a neck cushion

Use _____
When _____
Person _____

Use _____
When _____
Person _____

Use _____
When _____
Person _____

C. Work with another pair. Take turns talking about the inventions. Use this conversation to start but replace the highlighted parts with your own information. Decide which invention would be the most useful for your group.

A: *What do you think this is?*
B: *We think these could be eyedrops glasses.*
A: *OK. When would you use it, and who would find it useful?*
B: *You would use them to help you put in eyedrops, and people who can't put things in their eyes very well would find them useful.*
A: *So does that mean children could use them too?*

LESSON OBJECTIVES
▸ Recognizing weather information
▸ Understanding speakers' attitudes
▸ Expressing similarities and differences

Lesson 1 What's the summer like?

1 BEFORE YOU LISTEN

A. What is the weather like during the year in your country? Check (✓) the correct statements.

	Spring	Summer	Fall	Winter
1. It's hot and dry.	☐	☐	☐	☐
2. It's hot and humid.	☐	☐	☐	☐
3. It's rainy.	☐	☐	☐	☐
4. It's windy.	☐	☐	☐	☐
5. There is a little snow.	☐	☐	☐	☐
6. There is a lot of snow.	☐	☐	☐	☐
7. It's cold.	☐	☐	☐	☐
8. It's cool.	☐	☐	☐	☐
9. It's cloudy.	☐	☐	☐	☐
10. It's sunny.	☐	☐	☐	☐

B. What is your favorite season? Discuss with a partner.

2 LISTEN AND UNDERSTAND 🎧 CD 3 Track 18

A. A weather forecaster is describing the weather for cities around the world. What is the weather going to be like? Listen and check (✓) the correct columns.

	☀	🌧	❄	☁	🌬
1. Bangkok	☐	☐	☐	☐	☐
2. Chicago	☐	☐	☐	☐	☐
3. Miami	☐	☐	☐	☐	☐
4. Beijing	☐	☐	☐	☐	☐
5. London	☐	☐	☐	☐	☐

B. Listen again. What will the high temperature be in each city? Match each city with its correct temperature.

1. Bangkok ___	**a.** 29°
2. Chicago ___	**b.** 15°
3. Miami ___	**c.** 11°
4. Beijing ___	**d.** 36°
5. London ___	**e.** 2°

A. Friends are talking about how the weather affects them. Does it affect them in the same way or in a different way? Listen and ⟨circle⟩ the correct answer.

1. **a.** same   **b.** different
2. **a.** same   **b.** different
3. **a.** same   **b.** different
4. **a.** same   **b.** different

B. Listen again. How does the weather affect each person? Check (✓) the correct statement.

1. Sam
   a. He has little energy on rainy days. ____
   b. He gets up later in the winter. ____

2. Christina
   a. She does not like the snow. ____
   b. She likes cold weather. ____

3. Ken
   a. He does not like windy weather. ____
   b. He finds the winter difficult. ____

4. Young-jun
   a. He is active in the winter. ____
   b. He is happy in the summer. ____

④ **TUNE IN** 🎧 CD 3 Tracks 20 & 21

A. Listen and notice how people express similarities and differences.

	Similarities
A: *I feel much happier on sunny days than on rainy days.*	**B:** *Me too.* **B:** *Same with me.* **B:** *I'm just like you.* **B:** *I'm just the same.*
	Differences
A: *I enjoy cold weather, and I love the snow.*	**B:** *I'm just the opposite.* **B:** *I'm not like you at all.* **B:** *Not me.*

B. Now listen to other conversations. Does the person express a similarity or a difference in each conversation? Check (✓) the correct column.

	Similarity	Difference
1.	☐	☐
2.	☐	☐
3.	☐	☐
4.	☐	☐
5.	☐	☐
6.	☐	☐

⑤ AFTER YOU LISTEN

A. What do you think about the weather? Complete this survey for yourself. Check (✓) the statements that are true.

	Me	Student 1	Student 2
1. Rainy weather makes me depressed.	☐	☐	☐
2. I have more energy in the summer.	☐	☐	☐
3. I like cloudy days.	☐	☐	☐
4. I hate cold and dark days.	☐	☐	☐
5. Thunderstorms do not bother me.	☐	☐	☐
6. I have a lot of energy in the winter.	☐	☐	☐
7. I find it hard to get up in the winter.	☐	☐	☐
8. The weather affects my moods a lot.	☐	☐	☐
9. I cannot concentrate when it is very hot.	☐	☐	☐
10. I hate humid weather.	☐	☐	☐
11. I do not mind windy weather.	☐	☐	☐
12. I get allergies in the spring.	☐	☐	☐
13. Fall is my favorite season.	☐	☐	☐
14. I like it when it snows.	☐	☐	☐

B. Work in groups of three. Take turns making the statements and responding to them and complete the survey for your partners. Use this conversation to start but replace the highlighted parts with your own information. Which statements did you respond to in the same way?

A: *Rainy weather makes me depressed.*

B: *I'm not like you at all. I really like the rain.*

C: *I'm just like you. Rainy weather makes me sad.*

LESSON OBJECTIVES
▸ Identifying topics about the effects of weather
▸ Understanding sequences of events
▸ Showing interest

Lesson 2 What terrible weather we're having!

1 BEFORE YOU LISTEN

A. Match each weather event to the correct picture. Then compare your answers with a partner.

a.
b.
c.
d.
e.
f.
g.
h.

1. a thunderstorm ____
2. a hailstorm ____
3. a flood ____
4. a drought ____

5. a tornado ____
6. a typhoon ____
7. a snowstorm ____
8. fog ____

B. Circle the weather events in part A that happen where you live.

2 LISTEN AND UNDERSTAND 🎧 CD 3 Track 22

A. A class is talking about the way weather affects how houses are built. Which topic does the class talk about for each country? Listen and check (✓) the correct topic.

1. Cambodia
  a. what the houseboats are made of ____
  b. why some people live on houseboats ____

2. Oman
  a. why the houses have thick walls ____
  b. why the houses are big ____

3. Indonesia
  a. why the houses are built on poles ____
  b. what the weather in the summer is like ____

4. Austria
  a. why the houses are old ____
  b. how the roofs keep the snow off houses ____

B. Listen again. Are these statements true or false? Write *T* (true) or *F* (false).

1. There are floating schools in Cambodia. ____
2. The houses in Oman are cool at night. ____
3. Houses on poles are cooler than houses on the ground. ____
4. In Austria, the walls of houses are usually made of wood. ____

3 LISTEN AND UNDERSTAND 🎧 CD 3 Track 23

A. People are calling a radio show to talk about what happened to them during extreme weather. Listen and number the story events in the correct order.

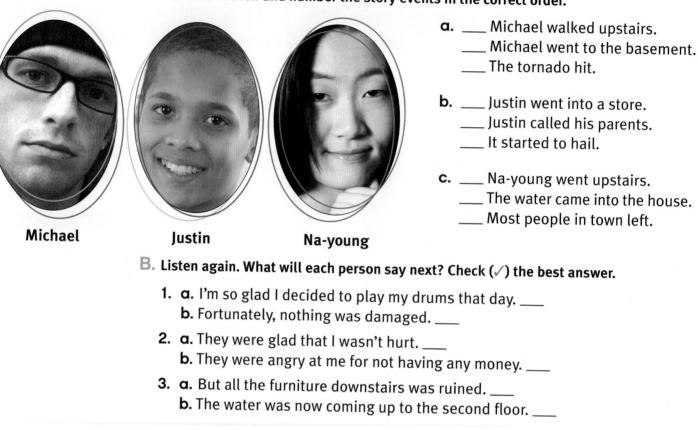

Michael   **Justin**   **Na-young**

a. ___ Michael walked upstairs.
___ Michael went to the basement.
___ The tornado hit.

b. ___ Justin went into a store.
___ Justin called his parents.
___ It started to hail.

c. ___ Na-young went upstairs.
___ The water came into the house.
___ Most people in town left.

B. Listen again. What will each person say next? Check (✓) the best answer.

1. a. I'm so glad I decided to play my drums that day. ___
b. Fortunately, nothing was damaged. ___

2. a. They were glad that I wasn't hurt. ___
b. They were angry at me for not having any money. ___

3. a. But all the furniture downstairs was ruined. ___
b. The water was now coming up to the second floor. ___

4 TUNE IN 🎧 CD 3 Tracks 24 & 25

A. Listen and notice how people show interest by using echo questions.

> **A:** *They even have schools on the water.*
> **B:** *Even schools?* That's amazing!
>
> **A:** *It gets very hot during the day, about 48 degrees.*
> **B:** *Forty-eight degrees?* Wow!
>
> **A:** *The pieces of ice were so big—as big as tennis balls.*
> **B:** *Tennis balls?* That's hard to believe!

B. Now circle the words a person might echo in each sentence. Then listen and check your answers.

1. It gets dark by four o'clock in the winter here.
2. In my country, we get snow for six months during the year.
3. When I was a kid, our house was destroyed by a typhoon.
4. It's really foggy where I live. We can get fog for over a 100 days a year.
5. Summer in New Zealand begins in December.
6. The temperature in my hometown is the same all year. It never changes.

5 AFTER YOU LISTEN

A. Read the statements in the Weather Quiz. (Circle) the four statements that are false.

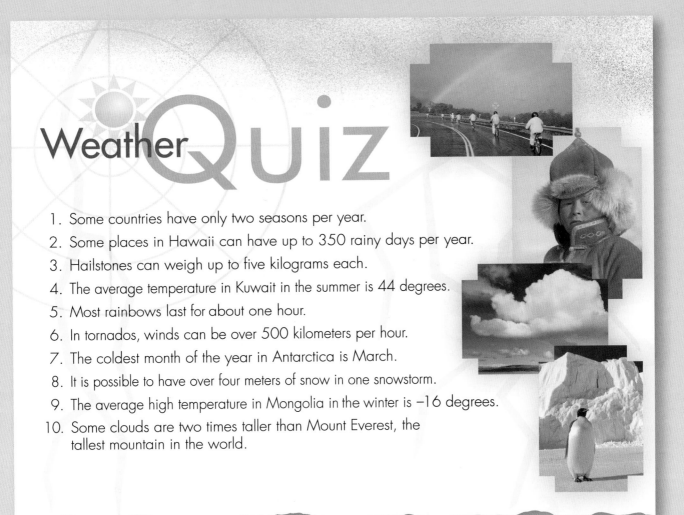

Weather Quiz

1. Some countries have only two seasons per year.
2. Some places in Hawaii can have up to 350 rainy days per year.
3. Hailstones can weigh up to five kilograms each.
4. The average temperature in Kuwait in the summer is 44 degrees.
5. Most rainbows last for about one hour.
6. In tornados, winds can be over 500 kilometers per hour.
7. The coldest month of the year in Antarctica is March.
8. It is possible to have over four meters of snow in one snowstorm.
9. The average high temperature in Mongolia in the winter is −16 degrees.
10. Some clouds are two times taller than Mount Everest, the tallest mountain in the world.

B. Work with a partner. Take turns making the statements and responding to them and compare your answers. Use this conversation to start but replace the highlighted parts with your own information. Then check your answers below.

A: "Some countries have only two seasons per year."
B: Two seasons per year? I think that's true. "Hawaii has up to 350 rainy days per year."
A: Three hundred and fifty rainy days per year? That's hard to believe. I think that's false . "Hailstones can weigh up to five kilograms each."
B: Five kilograms each? Wow, that's heavy. I think that's false.

C. Work with your partner. Decide which statement is the most surprising.

Answers: 3, 5, 7, 10 are false

Unit 14 Weekends

LESSON OBJECTIVES
▸ Identifying speakers' attitudes
▸ Understanding descriptions of events
▸ Responding to bad news

Lesson 1 How was your weekend?

1 BEFORE YOU LISTEN

A. What did you do last weekend? Check (✓) activities in the list and add two more of your own.

1. met someone interesting ___
2. bought something cool ___
3. helped as a volunteer ___
4. hung out with friends ___
5. went to the mall ___
6. went out to eat ___
7. worked part-time ___
8. slept in ___
9. _____
10. _____

B. Circle the statement that best describes your weekend. Then compare your answers with a partner.

1. It was fantastic!
2. It was nothing special.
3. It was nice.
4. It was a disaster.
5. It was OK.
6. It was depressing.

2 LISTEN AND UNDERSTAND 🎧 CD 3 Track 26

A. School friends are talking about their weekends. Were their weekends good, OK, or bad? Listen and check (✓) the correct column.

	Good	OK	Bad
1. Li-wei	☐	☐	☐
2. David	☐	☐	☐
3. Mark	☐	☐	☐
4. Hee-jin	☐	☐	☐
5. Richard	☐	☐	☐

B. Listen again. Are these statements true or false? Write *T* (true) or *F* (false).

1. Li-wei went to the mall on Sunday. ___
2. David was happy about the phone calls. ___
3. Mark was in a car accident. ___
4. Hee-jin got a job. ___
5. Richard watched a baseball game on TV. ___

③ LISTEN AND UNDERSTAND 🎧 CD 3 Track 27

A. Office coworkers are talking about their weekends. What did they do? Listen and check (✓) the statements that are true for each person.

	Victoria	Patrick	Henry	Keiko
1. did something for the first time	☐	☐	☐	☐
2. did something active	☐	☐	☐	☐
3. had a bad weekend	☐	☐	☐	☐
4. bought something	☐	☐	☐	☐
5. went somewhere with their parents	☐	☐	☐	☐
6. was happy with something they did	☐	☐	☐	☐

B. Listen again. What will each person ask next? Circle the correct question.

1. a. What did you have for breakfast?   **b.** Was it very cold up in the mountains?

2. a. What did you think of the movie?   **b.** Are you feeling better now?

3. a. Did you buy anything else?   **b.** How old is your sister?

4. a. Who did you play against?   **b.** Where did you buy it?

④ TUNE IN 🎧 CD 3 Tracks 28 & 29

A. Listen and notice how people respond to bad news.

> **A:** *My weekend was pretty awful, actually.*   **B:** *How come?*
> **A:** *My weekend was a disaster.*   **B:** *What do you mean?*
> **A:** *My weekend was terrible, actually.*   **B:** *Why was that?*

B. Now listen to other conversations. Is the person responding to good news or bad news in each conversation? Check (✓) the correct column.

	Good news	Bad news
1.	☐	☐
2.	☐	☐
3.	☐	☐
4.	☐	☐
5.	☐	☐
6.	☐	☐

A. Put these sentences in order to make two conversations. Then practice the conversations with a partner.

1.

____ I slipped on a banana peel in the subway and sprained my ankle.

____ Oh, that must have hurt.

____ It was terrible, actually.

____ How was your weekend?

____ Yeah, and then my mom made me go to the hospital.

____ Why was that?

____ Poor you!

2.

____ We couldn't agree on what DVD to rent.

____ How come?

____ No, not really. It was a disaster.

____ Did you have a good time on Saturday with your friend?

____ My friend and I had an argument. We're not talking now.

____ Oh, sorry to hear that. What was the argument about?

B. Work with a partner. What did you do two weekends ago? Write two activities. Then write two false activities.

1. _____

2. _____

3. _____

4. _____

C. Work with a partner. Take turns asking and answering questions about your weekends. Use this conversation to start but replace the highlighted parts with your own information. Guess which of your partner's activities are false.

A: *What did you do two weekends ago?*

B: *I went shopping with my mother, and she bought me new jeans.*

A: *Great! What else did you do?*

B: *Well, I also bought a new cell phone but left it on a bus the next day.*

A: *Hm, I think your mother bought you new jeans, but I don't think you bought and lost a new cell phone.*

B: *You're wrong!*

LESSON OBJECTIVES
▸ Identifying requests
▸ Understanding plans and decisions
▸ Using *something* or *anything*

Lesson 2 What are you doing this weekend?

1 BEFORE YOU LISTEN

What do you think of these events? Choose a statement in the box for each event. Then compare your answers with a partner.

That sounds like fun.	That could be interesting.	That sounds boring.
I've been to one before.	I think I'd like that.	I don't think I would enjoy that.

Electronics fair. See all the latest designs for everything from cell phones to laptops.

Book fair. Newest and best titles from the top publishers. 30% discount on all books.

Teen modeling competition. Help choose this year's top teen model.

Annual sale at the Mega Mall. Live entertainment, 30–40% off everything.

All-Asia pop concert. Top singers from Korea, Hong Kong, Taiwan, and Japan.

International food fair. Try great dishes from Mexico, Turkey, China, and other countries.

2 LISTEN AND UNDERSTAND 🎧 CD 3 Track 30

A. Friends have left voice-mail messages about weekend events. Listen and check (✓) the correct statement.

1. **a.** The festival is for one week. ___
   b. The festival is showing Marilyn Monroe movies. ___

2. **a.** The sale is for three days. ___
   b. Items are more than 50 percent off. ___

3. **a.** Jason wants to go skiing. ___
   b. The friends want to go to the mountains for a week. ___

4. **a.** The party is in the evening. ___
   b. The party is at a hotel. ___

5. **a.** Ben is planning to leave in the afternoon. ___
   b. The weather is going to be very hot. ___

B. Listen again. What does the person receiving the message need to do? Circle the correct answer.

1. **a.** go down to the cinema   **b.** look at a Website
2. **a.** call the store   **b.** call her friend
3. **a.** talk to his father   **b.** buy bus tickets
4. **a.** call her friend's cousin   **b.** go to her friend's house
5. **a.** take the bus   **b.** call his friend

3 LISTEN AND UNDERSTAND  CD 3 Track 31

A. Friends are talking about their plans for the weekend. What do they decide to do?
Listen and check (✓) the correct answer.

1. **a.** play tennis ___   **b.** go swimming ___
2. **a.** go shopping ___   **b.** go to the fair ___
3. **a.** go to the library ___   **b.** go skateboarding ___
4. **a.** watch TV ___   **b.** go to the stadium ___

B. Listen again. Why do the friends decide on their plan? Circle the correct answer.

1. **a.** no equipment   **b.** no time
2. **a.** no money   **b.** other plans
3. **a.** need to study   **b.** need a break
4. **a.** more convenient   **b.** more exciting

4 TUNE IN  CD 3 Tracks 32 & 33

A. Listen and notice how people use *something* or *anything* instead of giving a list of choices.

> **We use *something* with affirmative statements.**
> *I'd like to get out for some exercise or **something**.*
>
> **We use *anything* with negative statements.**
> *I'm not going out or **anything**.*
>
> **We use *something* or *anything* with questions.**
> *Do you want to go out or **something/anything**?*

B. Now circle *something*, *anything*, or both words to complete each sentence. Then listen and check your answers.

1. Let's see a movie or *something /anything* on Friday.
2. This weekend I'd really like to go for a picnic or *something /anything*.
3. Do you want to go for a drive or *something /anything* on Sunday?
4. I have to study this weekend. I can't go out or *something /anything*.
5. I can't go to the party on Saturday. I don't have a ride or *something /anything*.
6. Do you feel like going out for a hamburger or *something /anything*?

5 AFTER YOU LISTEN

A. You and your partner are planning to spend time together this weekend. Circle one activity in each box and add one activity of your own.

Nighttime activities	Daytime activities	Sports
go to a club	visit a friend	go for a long run
go see a movie	go shopping downtown	play tennis
eat at a restaurant	play computer games	go hiking
go to a friend's party	go to a museum	play basketball

Your own activity: _____

B. Which activities will you do and when will you do them? Take turns asking and answering questions about the activities you want to do. Use this conversation as a model. Then decide and write your weekend schedule.

A: *Do you want to go to a club or anything on Friday night?*

B: *Sure, that sounds good. I'd love to get out.*

A: *Let's go to that new one by school. I heard the music is really good there.*

B: *OK. What about Saturday afternoon? Do you want to go shopping or something?*

A: *No, not really. I don't want to be outside or anything. How about going to a museum?*

B: *That's a good idea. . .*

Friday	Saturday	Sunday
_____	_____	_____
_____	_____	_____
_____	_____	_____

C. Work with another pair. Take turns telling each other what you will do this weekend. Who will have the best weekend?

15 The News

LESSON OBJECTIVES
▸ Understanding news reports
▸ Understanding sequences of events
▸ Using intonation to make statements into questions

Lesson 1 What's in the news today?

1 BEFORE YOU LISTEN

What are these news reports about? Match each headline with its correct subhead. Then compare your answers with a partner.

1. Animal Lovers to the Rescue ___
2. Four-legged Hero ___
3. Wonder Kid ___
4. How to Reach a Century ___
5. A Quick Route to Prison ___
6. Vacation Horror ___

a. Living Long Through Healthy Dieting
b. Barking Dog Saves Man
c. Stupid Thieves Get Caught
d. Huge Fire Destroys Beach Resort
e. Five-Year-Old Pianist Wins Award
f. Saving Wild Birds in Danger

2 LISTEN AND UNDERSTAND 🎧 CD 3 Track 34

A. Reporters are choosing news stories. Listen and number the headlines for the stories from 1 to 4.

a. **Good Deed Leads to Traffic Delay** ___

c. **Healthy Living, Long Life** ___

b. **Time for a Well-Earned Bone** ___

d. Not on the Vacation Itinerary ___

B. Listen again. Circle the correct statement.

1. a. The same thing happens every year.
   b. The birds caused a traffic accident.
2. a. The women enjoy meat.
   b. The women have an unusual breakfast.
3. a. A fire broke out in the hotel.
   b. No one was injured.
4. a. The parents had gone out.
   b. The dog slept through the fire.

3 LISTEN AND UNDERSTAND 🎧 CD 3 Track 35

A. A news report is describing a bank robbery. Listen and number the events in the correct order.

____ The police arrested them.

____ They jumped into a car.

____ A bag broke open.

____ The armed men went into the bank.

____ They filled the bags with money.

____ They told everyone to lie down.

____ The car broke down.

____ They ran into a dead-end street.

B. Listen again. Are these statements true or false? Write *T* (true) or *F* (false).

1. There were three men. ____
2. The men took $8,000. ____
3. The bank opened just before the men came in. ____
4. The men filled two bags with money. ____
5. One of the men escaped. ____

4 TUNE IN 🎧 CD 3 Tracks 36 & 37

A. Listen and notice how people use rising intonation to make statements into questions.

A: *A group of bird lovers stop the traffic.*

B: *They actually hold up the traffic?*

A: *They're both still working on their vegetable farm.*

B: *They're both still active?*

A: *A helicopter lifted them out.*

B: *So they all got away safely?*

B. Now listen to other sentences. Are they statements or questions? Check (✓) the correct column.

	Statement	Question
1.	☐	☐
2.	☐	☐
3.	☐	☐
4.	☐	☐
5.	☐	☐
6.	☐	☐

5 AFTER YOU LISTEN

A. Match each story with two follow-up questions. Then practice the conversations with a partner.

1. Some children were playing in a park and found a wallet with $2,000 behind a bench. They gave it to the police. ___ ___

2. Scientists have finally found a cure for baldness. It contains a substance found in Chinese herbs. ___ ___

3. A man who was unemployed for five years won two million dollars in the lottery. It was the first lottery ticket he had ever bought. ___ ___

   a. He didn't have a job for five years?
   b. They actually gave all the money to the police?
   c. So he never bought a ticket before?
   d. It's only found in Chinese herbs?
   e. So the kids got a reward?
   f. It actually cures baldness?

B. Work with a partner. What happens in the story about the children who find $2,000 at a park? Talk about these pictures and write the rest of the story. How much money did the lady give the children as a reward?

1. Some children were playing in a park and found a wallet with $2,000 behind a bench.

2. They gave it to the police.

3. _____

4. _____

5. _____

6. _____

C. Work with another pair. Take turns telling each other your story. Are your stories different?

LESSON OBJECTIVES
▸ Understanding personal narratives
▸ Making inferences from key words
▸ Keeping stories going

Lesson 2 Tell me what happened

1 BEFORE YOU LISTEN

A. What do you think happened in these stories? Circle the correct statement for each picture. Then compare your answers with a partner.

1. a. She won a prize.
b. She got some bad news.

2. a. Her bag got stolen.
b. She lost her bag.

3. a. He cannot afford the bill.
b. He forgot his wallet.

B. Check (✓) the things that have happened to you recently. Then compare your answers with a partner.

1. You got good news. ___

2. Something made you embarrassed. ___

3. Something made you laugh. ___

4. Something frightened you. ___

2 LISTEN AND UNDERSTAND 🎧 CD 3 Track 38

A. People are telling stories about things that happened to them. Listen and number the story events in the correct order.

Story 1

___ She took a taxi.

___ She did not have much to do.

___ She went shopping.

___ She found some money.

___ She sat down to rest.

Story 2

___ They got into a helicopter.

___ They received free passes.

___ The wheel stopped.

___ They went on the Big Wheel.

___ They rode on rollercoasters.

B. Listen again. What will each person say next? Check (✓) the best answer.

Story 1
a. That was very kind of him. ___
b. That was a strange thing to do. ___
c. That was not very polite of you. ___

Story 2
a. When will you go again? ___
b. That was very rude of them. ___
c. It sounds like you had a really boring time. ___

3 LISTEN AND UNDERSTAND 🎧 CD 3 Track 39

A. People are telling stories about unusual experiences. Listen and number the story headings from 1 to 4.

a. A Difficult Problem ___   **c.** An Embarrassing Situation ___

b. A Bit of Good Luck ___   **d.** A Frightening Experience ___

B. Listen again. What probably happened next? Check (✓) the best answer.

1. **a.** He went back into the room. ___   **b.** He called the hotel lobby. ___
2. **a.** She went to collect her prize. ___   **b.** She threw away her ticket. ___
3. **a.** She ran downstairs. ___   **b.** She started playing with it. ___
4. **a.** He waited for the next car. ___   **b.** He threw away his phone. ___

4 TUNE IN 🎧 CD 3 Tracks 40 & 41

A. Listen and notice how people keep stories going by asking follow-up questions.

A: *I had a kind of interesting day on Sunday.*	B: *What happened?*
A: *They started getting people out by helicopter.*	B: *Then what happened?*
A: *My car broke down.*	B: *So then what did you do?*
A: *They called to say I had won.*	B: *What happened after that?*
A: *The spider jumped out of the box.*	B: *What happened next?*

B. Now listen to other conversations and number the follow-up questions you hear from 1 to 5.

a. What happened? ___

b. Then what happened? ___

c. So then what did you do? ___

d. What happened after that? ___

e. What happened next? ___

5 AFTER YOU LISTEN

A. Choose the correct questions in the box to complete the conversation. Then practice the conversation with a partner.

> Oh, no! Was she OK? What happened after that?
>
> How strange. Why did he laugh?
>
> That's a good costume. Was the party fun?
>
> So I guess things turned out OK in the end.
>
> Oh, really? What happened?
>
> How embarrassing! So then what did you do?

A: *Something really funny happened to me over the weekend.*

B: _____

A: *Well, a friend invited me to her costume party on Saturday night, and I decided to dress as a dog.*

B: _____

A: *Well, when I arrived at her house and rang the doorbell, the guy who answered started laughing at me.*

B: _____

A: *It wasn't a costume party! My friend changed her mind but forgot to tell me.*

B: _____

A: *I decided to enjoy myself anyway, but as I was getting a soda, I tripped and spilt my drink all over a girl.*

B: _____

A: *She started crying and left the party. All of her friends left too, so there were only five of us left. We started dancing and having fun then.*

B: _____

B. Work with a partner. What is the most embarrassing thing that could happen to you? Rank this list from 1 (most embarrassing) to 6 (least embarrassing).

____ You call your teacher *mom* or *dad* by mistake.

____ You walk into the wrong bathroom.

____ Someone finds your diary.

____ You do not have enough money to pay for the check at a restaurant.

____ You spill a drink on someone.

____ You forget your boyfriend's or girlfriend's name.

C. Work with another pair. Take turns telling each other your answers in part B. Give reasons for your answers. Did you rank the list in the same way?

Student CD Track List

This CD contains the final **Listen and Understand** of each lesson.

Track	Unit	Content
01		Title and copyright
02	Unit 1	Lesson 1, *page 3*
03		Lesson 2, *page 6*
04	Unit 2	Lesson 1, *page 9*
05		Lesson 2, *page 12*
06	Unit 3	Lesson 1, *page 15*
07		Lesson 2, *page 18*
08	Unit 4	Lesson 1, *page 21*
09		Lesson 2, *page 24*
10	Unit 5	Lesson 1, *page 27*
11		Lesson 2, *page 30*
12	Unit 6	Lesson 1, *page 33*
13		Lesson 2, *page 36*
14	Unit 7	Lesson 1, *page 39*
15		Lesson 2, *page 42*
16	Unit 8	Lesson 1, *page 45*
17		Lesson 2, *page 48*
18	Unit 9	Lesson 1, *page 51*
19		Lesson 2, *page 54*
20	Unit 10	Lesson 1, *page 57*
21		Lesson 2, *page 60*
22	Unit 11	Lesson 1, *page 63*
23		Lesson 2, *page 66*
24	Unit 12	Lesson 1, *page 69*
25		Lesson 2, *page 72*
26	Unit 13	Lesson 1, *page 75*
27		Lesson 2, *page 78*
28	Unit 14	Lesson 1, *page 81*
29		Lesson 2, *page 84*
30	Unit 15	Lesson 1, *page 87*
31		Lesson 2, *page 90*